HISTORY OF THE OLYMPIC GAMES

HISTORY OF THE OLYMPIC GAMES

FROM ANTIQUITY
TO THE
PRESENT TIME

CONSTANTINE L. SIRRACOS

Seaburn Publishing Group
P.O. Box 2085
LI, City NY 11102

ISBN 1-885778-53-8

Cover design by Andreas Kokkodis

1. INTRODUCTION

From the ancient times, man has in various ways expressed his natural inclination towards sporting activities. This inclination, which cultivates the competitive spirit, is based on such concepts as the enthousiasm for distinction, the admiration of excellence, the joy of victory, and the satisfaction of special feelings and ideals.

The involvement with athletic activities soon became one of the dominant forces in the lives of almost all people around the world and the sporting ideal found its best expression in modern times in the world-wide recognition and revival of the Olympic Games.

Greece, the cradle of western civilization, philosophy, science and democracy, was also the birthplace of the Olympic Games. In ancient Greece, sport constituted an inseparable part of every man's education. The Olympic spirit is the culmination of the ideal of education in ancient Greece, since it combined physical training, spiritual promotion, moral worth, democratic equality, and human brotherhood. It was here, in Greece, that the harmonious development of a man's body, mind and soul formed the ultimate ideal of human life.

The Olympic Games, which were the most important a-thletic games in ancient Greece, reflect the immortal spirit of Greece that aims at promoting the human "kallos", a Greek word meaning in fact the sum total of the attributes of morality, justice, beauty of body and mind, and involvement with higher sentiments and ideas.

It is of utmost importance that the Games be kept away from politics and vested interests and remain a world-wide human expression of friendship, peace and love; a unique event during which language, race and religion barriers no longer exist; an event in which social position and material wealth play no role in determining an individual's respect and admiration.

It is the present author's view that in order to keep political and other differences out of the Olympic Games and, therefore, in order to prevent the Games from becoming platforms on which athletic ideals will be sacrificed for political expediency, a tendency that will inevitably kill the Olympic idea, the Games should take place on a permanent site that would be located in the birth-place of the Olympic ideal: in ancient Olympia.

1.1. The Athletic Spirit in the antiquity

To the immense fertility of the ancient Greek mind belongs the development of the athletic ideal that found its expression, during the 5th century B.C., in the great panhellenic sanctuaries of Olympia, Delphi, Isthmus and Nemea.

The athletic activity resulted naturally from the innate human tendency of moving around. It is an activity that involves the body, the mind and the soul. It promotes both individuality and the collective spirit, depending on whether it is performed individually or in the context of a team. The athlete learns to compete, to fight, to win and, most importantly, to lose. Below, we present an extract from a book, by G. Sakellariou, a former director of the National Academy of Physical Training, entitled "Greece and Athletics" (1947).

"It is true that dances, games, athletic events and contests have been developed by all peoples in the world. However, it seems that only in Greece has the real physical training or gymnastics risen to the level not of simple ceremony but of an activity that intends to lead the human mind to a higher sphere of intellectual, aesthetic, social and political content".

2. ATHLETIC CONTESTS IN ANCIENT GREECE

2.1. An Overview

The first country the placed emphasis on sports was Greece. In ancient Greece, sport formed an integral part of a man's education. The Greeks had very clearly conceived

A shell-shaped jumping-weight (a "halter", in Greek). The jumpers used such "halteres" in order to gain impetus, balance their position in the air and, therefore, improve their performance. The stone jumping weight presented above was, according to the relevant inscription, a thanksgiving dedication of Akmatidas of Sparta, winner of the pentathlon. (Olympia, Archaeological Museum).

that physical education contributed to human health and to the balanced development of body and soul. As a result, every Greek city had built its own *gymnasia* (gymnastic schools) which attracted not only the youth, but practically all citizens. The youths of Athens spent a significant part of their childhood and adolescence in the *gymnasia* which were also frequented by older men.

Every Greek city held gymnastic and religious festivities. These festivities were devoted to the honor of a specific god who was believed to protect the city. The Greeks believed that their gods loved joy and festivals. Therefore, in order to please the gods, the youths sang and danced around the gods' altars.

Also, in order to amuse the honored god, they used to organize athletic contests such as running, wrestling and jumping.

The sense of and the need for competition was so inextricably bound up with the lives of the Greeks that *Agon,* the Greek word for competition, contest, had been personified and represented in various forms. According to Pausanias, a statue of *Agon* holding jumping weights in his hands was erected in the sanctuary of Olympia. Also, there were representations of *Agon* on the gold and ivory table on which the crowns which were to be given to the winners of the Olympic Games were laid.

In addition it should be noted that the word *Agon* in ancient Greek means also gathering of people, congregation. As the gods of the Greeks were believed to have human attributes, it was thought that the gods became happier the bigger the crowd. Likewise, the gods were assumed to become extremely happy at the sight of the well-trained bodies of the athletes.

2.2. Games performed

According to tradition and as show relevant excavations, the Greeks had established various games. The
origin of the athletic contests is actually lost in the unclear
mist of prehistoric times and mythology. Some of the
myths surrounding the history of the athletic contests are

Panathenaic amphora   Stadion runners

mutually exclusive, others contradict reality and still
others are supported by undisputed archaeological
evidence.

The Greek myths seem invariably to suggest that most,
if not all, games were established in honor of a dead hero,
a semi-god, or a god. Thus we see that the Cretans in the
Minoan period, in the third and second millennium B.C.,
and later the Achaeans during the Trojan War, exercised in
running, rowing, discus throwing, wrestling, etc.

The love of contest is also predominant in Homer's Odyssey. There we learn that Alkinoos, the king òf the Phaiakians, held games in order to honor Odysseus. Also, in Homer's *Iliad* we see that Achilles organized games to honor his dead friend Patroclos, killed by Hector during the Trojan War. The contests described in the *Iliad* in the funeral games held in honor of Patroclos were the following: chariot racing won by Diomedes; boxing won by Epeios; wrestling won by Ajax; running won by Odysseus; and archery won by Meriones.

Also, the Spartans held athletic contests in order to honor Leonidas and the three hundred who fell in Thermopylai, in the great battle with the Persians.

Although the ancient Greeks had instituted many games, four of these went beyond the bound of the strictly local and acquired Panhellenic character and importance: the Olympic games which were held at Olympia; the Pythian games held at Delphi, propably Greece's most eminent sanctuary; the Isthmian games held at the Isthmus; and the Nemean games held at Nemea. Needless to say that the most brilliant and famous of the above were the Olympic games. Below, we present the highlights of the Nemean, Isthmian and Pythian games.

The Pythian games were, according to the prevailing tradition, established by Appolo, the god of the Delphic sanctuary, after he had slain the *Python*. It is believed that the first games had the form of a musical contest. The games were reorganized by the tyrrant Kallisthenes of Sykyon who added to the musical contest gymnastic games along the lines of the Olympic games. Also, Kallisthenes decided that from that date (586 B.C.) the games should be held every four rather than every two years that was the practice until then.

The prize that went to the winners of the events was a crown of laurel. The Panhellenic nature of the Pythian games has been verified by various sources. The end of the Pythian games came in 394 A.D. as a result of the famous edict of emperor Theodosius and coincided with the end of the Olympic games.

The origin of the Nemean games is a subject that has given rise to controversy, as the existing evidence is far from conclusive. However, the prevailing view seems to suggest that the Nemean games were funeral games in honor of the seven general who had campaigned against the city of Thebes. These games were held every two years in the valley of Nemea. Some of the most famous winners of the first Nemean games were the following: Eteoklis in running, Polynikis in wrestling, Tydeus in boxing, Amphiaraos in jumping, Adrastos in chariot racing, Parthenopaios in archery and Laodokis in javelin.

Although the exact beginning of these games cannot be identified with accuracy, ancient sources suggest 571 B.C. as the first year of the games. However, the official counting of the Nemean games began in 500 B.C. For purposes of comparison the reader should be reminded that the official counting of the Olympic games began in 776 B.C.

The winners of the Nemean games were given a crown of celery, a plant associated with the dead and therefore was in tune with the fact that the Nemean games were funeral games.

Another tradition relates the Nemean games to the myth of the Nemean lion killed by Herakles.

The Isthmian games turned out to be the next most important Panhellenic games after the Olympic games. According to the prevailing tradition, which is further supported by archaiological evidence, the Isthmian games, which were held every two years at the Isthmus of Corinth at the sanctuary of the god Poseidon, were founded by Sisyphos as funeral games in honor of the drowned hero Meli kertes and dedicated to both Poseidon and Melikertes.

The ancient Greeks began to count officially the Isthmian games from 583 B.C. The winners of the games were given a branch of pine.

Other local games that deserve to be mentioned here were the following:

The Panathenaia which were held in honor of Athena, the tutelary godess of the city of Athens; the Herakleia in Marathon; the Helloteika at Korinth; the Alkatheia at Megara; the Didymeia at Miletos; the Heraia at Argos; the Naia at Dodoni; the Asclepeia at Epidavros; the Herakleia at Thebes; the Erotideia at Thespiae in honor of the god Apollo, and others.

It seems fair to say that for the ancient Greeks the running race was considered as the most important athletic competition. Some of the most famous runners were Argeus, Pheidippides, Polymmestos and Euchidas.

Other popular events were wrestling, boxing, the pankration which can be described as a combination of wrestling and boxing, the Pentathlon which included jumping, running, javelin, wrestling and discus, and some equestrial events like chariot racing and horse racing.

Events of rather minor importance and popularity were archery, torch racing and swimming. Finally, it should be mentioned in this brief account that the event of armed combat (in Greek oplomachia) in which the competitors engaged in mock fights and displayed formally the methods of real warfare, did not flourish in Greece during the peak of the Greek civilization but became popular later, during the Hellenistic period.

We should also mention that the ancient Greek games included artistic contests.

2.3. Kinds of ancient Greek games

As we have already implied, the institution and periodic holding of athletic games in ancient Greece was the result of a variety of factors and influences. Very often games were instituted in order to commemorate some special event. The facility with which the Greeks used to take the decision to hold games can be explained on the grounds that the Greeks would seize every opportunity to express their competitive spirit and to develop it into an athletic ideal. We already saw that the king of the Phaiakians held games to honor Odysseus. Further, in order to commemorate the defeat of the Persians, the Greeks instituted the Elefthereia games which were held in Plataia. Also, in order to honor dead heroes, the ancient Greeks used to hold funeral games. Homer, in the 23rd rapsody of his *Iliad* describes in detail the funeral games held in honor of Patroklos. Further, we know from the same source that funeral games were held for Amarynkeas at Bouprasinon in Elis. Finally, funeral games are known to have been held after the death of the tyrant Oedipus.

In addition, the Greeks held games in order to express gratitude to the Gods, especially after military victories, while other games were associated with the fertility of the land.

In some cases a husband was chosen through athletic

15

Marble statue depicting a stadion girl runner. Greek Art of the 5th century B.C.

16

contests, according to Greek myths. Thus, Atalante had declared that she would marry the first man who would defeat her in a race. She competed with her suitors and defeated a large number of them until she was beaten by Hippomenes and became his wife.

Similarly, Oinomaos, king of Pisa, held a famous chariot race in order to choose the husband for his daughter Hippodameia. As a result, Pelops married Hippodameia after defeating his competitors in the chariot race. Likewise, Ikarios gave Penelope to Odysseus after Odysseus had beaten all the other aspiring suitors in a race. Further, Danaos held games to choose husbands for his 50 daughters.

According to a myth Endymion, the king of Elis, held a contest in order to decide the successor to his throne among his three sons. Other games, like the Panionia were held jointly by the twelve Ionian cities of Asia Minor for political reasons, specifically in order to consolidate the unity of the cities and to take political decisions of mutual interest.

2.4. The participation of women at the games

As a rule the women were not allowed to take part in the games. Furthermore they were not permitted even to watch the games as spectators. However in certain cities women could participate in specified athletic events. In this context we should state that the Dorians and the Aeoleis were much more liberal than the Ionians who believed that women should stay at home and look after the children and the house. By sharp contrast, the Heleans held special games for girls, the Heraia, in honor of the

A virgin winner of the "Heraia". Ancient Greek statue in the Vatican.

godess Hera. The prevailing tradition says that the Heraia, which took place in the stadium of Olympia, were completely independent of the Olympic games. The Heraia were established by Hippodameia after her marriage to Pelops. The girls were divided into three categories on the basis of their age, namely children, adolescents and young women. They competed only in one event, running, which roughly corresponds to the modern event of women's 200 meters. According to Pausanias, the winners were given a crown of olive and a piece of the cow that was sacrificed to Hera. The girls did not compete completely naked, as did the men, but wore a short dress (chiton, in Greek) which left their right shoulder uncovered to the breast.

2.5. Honors conferred to the victors and importance attached to the games

Originally, the awards that were given to the victors were valuable objects. In later times, the victors used to go to the temple of the patron deity of their cities and dedicate the awards to the god. Alternatively, they used to dedicate their awards to the sanctuary of the place in which the games were held. Still later, the habit of crowning the victors was established. The crowns were made from *kotinos* (wild olive), laurel, myrtle, pine, palm, celery e.t.c.

Victory at the Olympic games was the highest glory and the highest honor to which an individual could attain. Ancient sources tell us that during the 113th Olympiad the crowned athlete Argeus ran a distance of one hundred kilometers immediately after his crowning, in order to announce his victory to his city, Argos.

Also, Chelon of Lakedaemon died from a heart attack caused by intense emotion, as soon as he embraced his crowned son who had won the boxing contest. So great was the honor attributed to the victors and the significance and prestige of the Games that the Greeks linked their worship of the gods with the holding of games. Further, in their legends associated the origins of the games with their gods and heroes. Almost every event was believed to have been invented by a god or hero. For example, Jason was supposed to have invented the Pentathlon and Apollo the boxing event. The gods were assumed even to compete in athletic games. Thus, Zeus, the father of all gods wrestled with and defeated Kronos at Olympia, while Apollo beat Hermes in running and Ares in boxing. Even Kastor and Polydeukes were regarded as Olympic victors, while the victory of the Greeks over the Persians was seen as equal to an Olympic victory. We feel that the above brief description gives the reader a good idea of the enormous esteem to which the ancient Greeks held the Games.

3. OLYMPIA

3.1. Origin of the name

The ancient Olympia was not a city. It was the oldest and one of the two most prestigious sanctuaries of Greece, the other being the sanctuary of Delphi. The complex of the sanctuary and the other buildings are located in the valley of the Alpheios river in the western Peloponese. The sanctuary extends over the foot of the Kronion hill, between the rivers Alpheios and Kladeos. Today, in the area of the antiquities there is a small town also called Olympia. This modern town, however, has no historical or other link with the ancient Olympia, which was never inhabited by permanent residents. In particular, Olympia was a religious center resempling a modern monastery, a remote religious commune that turned out to be a most prestigious religious center for the Hellenic world.

3.2. Location

The ancient Olympia lies in the north-western side of

Kronion or Kronios hill. The cone-shaped hill, north of the Temple of Zeus. It is said that during the mythical times this hill was dedicated to the worship of god Kronos.

The valley of Olympia, run by the silvery water of the river Alpheios.

Peloponese, 19 miles from the city of Pyrgos, the capital of the province of Ilia. The sanctuary thrived in the lush valley of the Alpheios river. This place was chosen for the holding of the most famous athletic event of the ancient Greek world, the Olympic Games. In the area of the sanctuary there were temples, tombs, altars, statues and exquisite artifacts. Also there were a number of buildings designed for the athletes and the people in charge of the conduct of the Games, a kind of modern Olympic village.

3.3. Altis

Altis means grove, and, more specifically, sacred grove. By Altis we refer to the sacred grove of Olympia, which during the 7th century B.C. was covered with plane

ALTIS (its present-day ruins)
Altis means sacred grove dedicated to the worship of gods.

trees, wild olives, poplar trees, oaks, pines and, especially, palm trees.

The Altis was enclosed by a low encircling wall. Within the Altis there were a few buildings such as altars to the gods and shrines.

It seems right to say that the ancient Greeks could not have chosen a better site for the establishment of the sanctuary of Olympia. It is an environment most couducive to the development of the human soul and body.

3.4. Establishment of the first sanctuaries

The exact date of the establishment of the first sanctuaries is not known. Before the Dorian invasion the area of the sanctuary and its environs belonged to the city of ancient Pisa. The Pisatans were Achaeans and are known to have been the first inhabitants of Ilis. It was they who established the sancuary referred to as "Gaion".

In the same place pre-existed an altar and an oracle dedicated to Zeus. Subsequently, the Pisatans erected on the summit of the mountain overlooking Olympia an altar to Kronos, son of Uranus and Earth, thus naming the mountain Kronion.

An alternative tradition has it that the first inhabitants of Ilis were the Pelasgi, who also established the sanctuaries.

According to a view, the name Olympia is prehellenic, deriving from the word Olympos, meaning mountain. Still another view claims that the sacred area took its name from the Olympian Zeus, the father of all gods and humans; it was for the honor of the Olympian Zeus that the Games were called Olympic Games.

Reproduction of the sanctuary of Olympia.

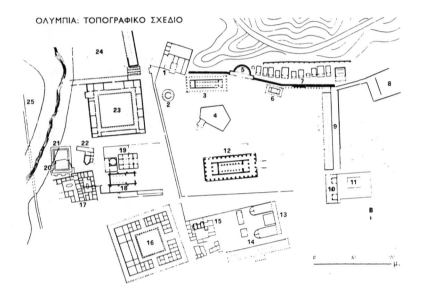

OLYMPIA: Topographical plan.
1 - Prytaneion. 2 - Philippeion. 3 - Heraion. 4 - Pelopeion. 5 - Nymphaion. 6 - Metroon. 7 - Area of the Treasuries. 8 - Stadium. 9 - Stoa of Echo. 10 - Northeastern building. 11 - House of Nero. 12 - Temple of Zeus. 13 - Bouleuterion. 14 - South Stoa. 15 - Thermai. 16 - Leonidaion. 17 - Roman guest-houses. 18 - Workshop of Pheidia. 19 - Theokoleon. 20 - Thermai of Kladeos. 21 - Aqueduct. 22 - Baths of the classical era. 23 - Palaistra. 24 - Gygmansion. 25 - Wall.

From the beginning of the second millenium B.C. the area of Olympia was dedicated to the worship of the earth and the forces of fertility. As a result, the sanctuary attracted the interest of the new conquerors the Elians who subjected and ousted the Pisatans and the Epeians in the 12th century, that is at the time of the Dorian invasion. Subsequently the valley was named Elis.

Ancient Palaistra. Imaginary reconstruction.

The authority and strength of Elis was significantly diminished during the 7th century B.C. In a number of ill-fated battles Elis conceded much of the territory it had acquired during the previous centuries.

In the early 6th century B.C. Elis recovered its power and imposed the worship of Zeus.

Having renewed its strength, Elis, helpled by Sparta, dealt a decisive blow to Pisa and resumed its control of the sanctuary, which it retained ever since until the Games ceased to be held.

From the early Archaic times, all the Greeks participated in the activities of the sanctuary. With the passage of time, the sanctuary became increasingly important and attracted Greeks not only from the mainland but also from Asia Minor, the Black Spa, and the Mediterranean colonies. New buildings were erected and the sanctuary of Olympia takes gradually the form of the most important religious center of the Greek world.

3.5. Olympia as a panhellenic athletic center

Ancient Olympia was the region chosen by the ancient Greeks as a place for the worship of all gods, and in particular of Zeus, in whose honor an altar had been constructed. In all probability, the religious congregation of thousands of people around the sanctuaries of Olympia, was the principal reason for the creation of The Olympia, the most celerated athletic events. These events turned the place of Olympia into a panhellenic and, one could claim, a world center of that era.

The Olympia were instituted in the 7th century B.C., took place in the summer, every four years, and caused the attendance of unimaginable crowds not only from continental Greece, but also from the Greek colonies in Italy, Sicily, various other places along the coasts of the Mediterranean Sea and even in Asia Minor.

Dorians, Ionians, Athenias, Spartans and Thebans, regardless of their differences and even if they happened to be in a state of war, would immediately agree a ceasefire and go to Olympia for the Games. The Olympia constituted the most sacred celebration of Greece.

The honors that were conferred to the victors of the Olympic Games were considered to be the highest possible human glory and achievement. Nothing could be thought of to represent an acquisition as important as the wild-olive crown of the Olympic victory. Kings from remote Kyrene, tyrants from Sicily princes from the powerful aristocracies of Corinth, Argos and Thessaly, rich men from

Imaginary reconstruction of an Olympic foot-race.

everywhere, fought to win the Olympic crown of honor which would give the immortal glory.

Neither the dangers and fatigue of long-distance travel, nor the possibility of a foreign invasion thwarted the zeal of the Greeks to attend the Olympic Games.

It is notable that while Leonidas, the King of Sparta, was fighting to stop the Persian invasion in Thermopylai, the Greeks were celebrating another Olympiad, unwilling to put off the Games because of the war.

From Olympia, this panhellenic sporting hub, passed during the twelve centuries that the Games spanned, scores of emperors, kings, statesmen, philosophers, writers, poets and artists.

3.6. Introduction to the Olympic spirit

The sacred place that is called Olympia has been the most famous in the whole of Greece. It was the greatest religious center in antiquity and still has a good number of statues. There was also a temple erected to honor Zeus.

Thanks to the establishment of the Olympic Games that took place regularly from 776 B.C. until 393 A.D., Olympia grew into the most important athletic center of Greece.

Olympia became a symbol, an idea.

The Olympic Games represented the symbol of Greek brotherhood. The radiance of the Games attracted the interest and devotion of all Greeks.

For twelve centuries Olympia was the place in which the most important athletic attainments were performed and in modern times gave its glorious name to the new Olympic Games.

4. THE OLYMPIC GAMES IN THE ANTIQUITY

4.1. Foundation of the Olympic Games

The exact date of the first Olympic Games that took place in Ancient Greece is not known. The beginning of the Games is lost in the dark mist of early history. As a result, the institution of the Games has been connected with various mythological traditions. One of these traditions relates the beginning of the Games to the wrestling between Jupiter and Zeus in order to settle the question of world domination. In this contest, Zeus, who then was a child, invited his father to wrestle with him in the valley of Elis.

The fight took place in the ravines of Kyllene and Erymanthos, far from the indiscreet eyes of the mortals. Zeus emerged as the victor of the contest. Later, in order to celebrate this great victory, the Greeks organized athletic contests in the plains of Olympia. Among the first competitors of these contests was Apollo, who beat Mercury in a running event and Mars in pugilism, thus being named an Olympic Victor.

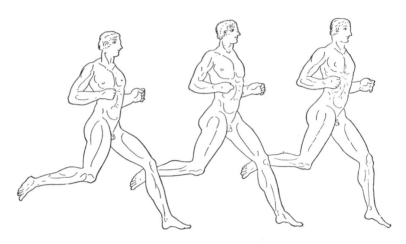

Dolichos runners. A representation on an ancient vase.

According to another myth, the founder of the Games was Hercules, the son of Zeus. It was Hercules who first determined the length of the Olympic stadium (600 feet) and the limits of the Altis that was dedicated to Zeus.

Another story has it that founder of the Games was the Idaian Herakles, the older of the Kouretes brothers, or Idaian Daktyloi, who was believed to have brought the sacred olive tree from the Hypernortherners. The Kouretes were Cretan fighters and priests who lived in Idi, a small town in Krete. In this town existed a castle in which the Kouretes brought up Zeus. In particular, Zeus was kept in hiding from his father Jupiter who was searching for the baby Zeus to kill him. The Kouretes brought Zeus from Krete to Peloponese, in the valley of Alfeios. In order to keep the baby's cries from being heard by Jupiter, the Kouretes kept banging their metalic shields. The artifice worked and, subsequently, Herakles suggested the establishment of a running contest to commemorate the rescue of Zeus. The winner of the race would be awarded a wild-olive crown (kotinos). The winner of the race was Herakles who was then given the crown. The above event contributed to the establishment of Games every five years. The five-year interval between consecutive games was related to the fact the Idaian Kouretes were five brothers.

Another myth relates the establishment of the Olympic Games with Aegeas, while another tradition refers to the Theban Herakles as the founder of the Games. The latter, after one of his famous exploits, namely the cleansing the palace of Avgeas, king of Elis, held Games in Olympia to commemorate his achievement. A further myth, mentions the name of Aethlios, a son of Zeus and Protogeneia (daughter of Defkalion). Aethlios was supposed to be the first king of Elis, according to the mythology. From

The synthesis of the east pediment of the temple of Zeus refers to the mythical chariot race between the king of Pisa Oinomaos and the young Pelops. The winner of the race, Pelops, married Oinomaos' daughter Hippodameia. Zeus is depicted in the middle of the actors of the myth. In particular, Oinomaos with his wife Sterope appears on the right of Zeus, and Pelops with Hippodameia on the left of Zeus.

his name, the participants of sporting events were called athletes.

A generation before Pelops, Endymion, son of Kalike and Aethlios and second king of Elis, organized a running race among his children Paion, Epeios, and Aetolos, Epeios won the race and succeeded his father to the throne. Later, Eleios succeeded Epeios and named the region Eleia. The first-born Paeon, disappointed by his defeat, left for Macedonia and lived in the region that later was called Paeonia.

Still another view claims that the real founder of the Olympic Games was Pelops, son of the king of Frygia Tantalos, who with the help of Poseidon and the bribery of Myrtilos, Oinomaos's charioteer, managed to win the now celebrated chariot race from Olympia to Corinth, and married Hippodameia.

Finally, the major founder of the Games seems to have been the single-eyed Aetolos Oxylos who arrived in Elis with the Dorian invaders in 1104 B.C. Iphitos, a descendant of Oxylos can be surely regarded as the man who actually organized and established the Olympic Games. This fact seems to be confirmed by the treaty signed by Ifitos, king of Eleia, Kleosthenes, king of Pisa, and the Spartan Lykourgos, in 884 B.C. According to this treaty, the region of Elis is ceclared a sacrosanct area during the holding of the Games, even during wars.

The agreement of the truce, "ekehereia" in Greek, was engraved on a disk made from copper. The historian and peregrinator Pausanias testified that he read the truce agreement when he visited the temple of Hera, in Olympia.

The truce was only once violated by a Spartan warrior. As a result, Sparta paid the Heleans a heavy financial penalty.

34

4.2. Participation in the games

In 776 B.C., when Iphitos, king of Elis reorganized the Olympic Games, he put into effect a grand design for the best use of the insitution. By making peace with Sparta and Pisa, he helped bring about the establishment of the panhellenic "ekecheiria" (truce). The "ekecheria" was a sacred armistice that was extended to any Greek city that wished to participate in the Games.

As a result, during the Games there was a suspension of hostilities for a prescribed period, and the athletes and spectators could easily and safely participate in the Games.

The announcement of the Games was made by heralds who travelled throughout Greece to invite the athletes and the spectators to go to Olympia.

Participation in the Olympic Games was not open to all In particular, the athletes had to be Greeks. This meant that foreigners and slaves were not allowed to take part. Also, all those who had been found guilty of murder or robbing a temple were excluded from the Games. Further, the married women were not allowed to participate, with the exception of the priestess of Demeter Chamyne. Also, those who had for same reason lost their political rights, were excluded from the Games. The Spartans were excluded from the Games of 420 B.C. because they had violated the sacred truce. Also, the Athenians were once denied participation becuase they refused to pay a financial penalty.

4.3. Organization of the games — ekechereia

The entire organization and supervision of the Games was the responsibility of the Elean Hellanodikai who were riginally two and later twelve. As the time of the Games approached, the spondophoroi, heralds from Olympia, travelled all over Greece to proclaim the Olympian ekechereia, the sacred truce. The truce initially lasted one month and later three months. During the truce, all hostilities ceased and the best athletes went to Olympia to train under the supervision of the Elean judges.

It is fair to say that the sacred truce, which was instituted by Iphitos as a way to prevent Greece from being torn out by civil war, was the gratest pacifist achivment of the antiquity.

The Greeks later personified the ekechereia, representing a woman crowing Iphitos.

During the truce, all those who wished to attend or take part in the Games were free to travel even through areas with which their own country was at war. Further, no armed person or armies were allowed to enter Elis. Finally, all death penalties were suspended during the sarced truce.

There is some uncertaintly regarding the exact date of the Olympic Games. In all probability, however, the Games were held at the first full moon after the summer solstice, and historians today seem to agree that they were held in July.

4.4. Hellanodikai

The "Hellanodikai" of Olympia were responsible for the conduct of the Games. They were alternatively called "agonothetai". They were entitled to impose financial and plysical penalties and to eliminate athletes from the Games. One of their tasks was to award the prizes. They judged according to the existing laws and their verdicts were respected and irrevocable. We may accurately say that the Hellanodikai constituted the highest political authority in Elis.

The Hellanodikai were selected from those Eleans who had experience of athletics. They held office for a period of ten months. In particular, they were appointed ten months before the commencement of the Games and their service expired at the end of the Olympiad.

The Hellanodikai lived in the Hellanodikaion, a specially built structure near the agora of Elis. There, they received instruction in their duties and in the rules and regulations governing the conduct of the Games. Their teachers were called "nomophylakes" that is observers of the laws. At the same time they supervised the training of the athletes, improved their theoretical knowledge, recorded the names of the athletes that were to take part in the constests and, in general, organized and administered the festivities associated with the Olympic Games.

For reasons of objectivity, the Hellanodikai were required to take an oath, promising to give impartial verdicts.

The Hellanodikai during the Games wore purple cloaks and a laurel wreath.

Initially there was only one judge (Hellanodikes) of the Games. However, later their number increased to two, as a result of the increase in the number of the events. Both were selected from among the noble families of Elis.

Because the Eleans wanted the Games to remain respectable and auhtoritative athletic events, they took every care to make sure that the rules were strictly observed and the judges absolutely impartial.

The Pisatans who for years wanted to take over the organization of the Games succeeded in assuming the presidency of the eighth Olympiad (748 B.C.) with the assistance of the tyrant of Argos, Phidon, and again later, during the 34th Olympiad under the leadership of Pisa's king Pantaleon.

Finally, in 580 B.C., the Eleans conquered and destroyed Pisa and subsequently remained the sole judges and supervisors of the Games.

From 480 B.C. (75th Olympiad) onwards, the number of Hellanodikai was increased to nine, of whom three supervised the equestrian events, three the pentathlon, and three the other events. Later the Hellanodikai became ten and still later twelve.

4.5. Preparation and commencement of the games

At least one month before the beginning of the Games, the athletes arrived in Olympia and began training themselves daily and systematically. For their training, the Gymnasion and the Wrestling place were built.

Ten months before the beginning of each Olympiad the Hellanodikai used to assume their duties which consisted mainly of attending, supervising and teaching the training of the athletes. In this way, the Hellanodikai obtained valuable experience that helped them improve the quality of their work.

Three months before the Games, the heralds of Olympia travelled through Greece and announced the sacred ekecheria (truce). The heralds were the eight chairmen of the Games. Subsequently the terms of the truce were pulbished and all hostilities were suspended.

The Games were held at the first full moon following the summer solstice, that is at the beginning of the summer.

With the sunrise of the official commencement day, the

Hellanodikai or Judges took their seats. The stadium was full of people, both athletes and sperctators. All sorts of people, artists, merchants, and simple pilgrims used to go to Olympia to watch the Games. All over the valley one could hear the noise made by the charlots, the singers, the people etc. The whole countryside echoed with voices, songs and laughter.

Suddenly, under conditions of absolute silence, the head of the Hellanodikai asked his collegues and the athletes to follow him in procession to the Temple of Zeus. There, the priests, surrounded by the officials killed animals as a sacrifice to Zeus. Then the competitors swore that they had trained for the previous the months in accordance with the rules and that they would not commit any unfair method to win, that is they would not violate the rules of the Games. Also the judges who used to assist the Hellabodikai swore that they would judge impartially and would keep their decisions secret.

Then, the Hellanodikai, the officials and the sperctators took their places in the Stadium. Subsequently the head of the Hellanodikai rose to his feet, raised the palmbranch that he used to hold high, the trumpeter blew his trumpet and the herald announced the Games open.

Immediately afterwards, the herald called the competitors to come forward. The athletes lined up and then the herald asked in a loud voice if there was anyone who could charge any competitor with violating the laws of the country. It is interesting to know that during the long life of the Games no athlete had ever been charged with any violation of the law. This shows that so great was the respect for the Games that no lawbreaker would even dare appear in the Olympics.

4.6. The Olympic Events

The first established Olympic event is considered to be the cariot racing. The chariot races began in the pregeometric period in honor of Pelops near his tomb which was called "the Pelopion". In 776 B.C. the only chariot race event was replaced by a type of foot-race event, the "stadion" (1 stade = 192.27 meters).

Running was the earliest and most natural of the events

Pankratiasts. Statue in the Museum of Florence.

contested in Olympia. Winners in running events were thought to enjoy a special distinction because running was of special importance throughout the whole of antiquity. As a result, each Olympiad took its name from the winner in the stadion race.

During the Olympiad of 776 B.C. the victor was Koroibos of Elis, whose name was engraved for the first time on the list of the Olympic victors.

Pankratiasts.

The stadion race was the only foot-race event until the 14th Olympiad (724 B.C.), when the "diavlos" event, that included two lengths of the track, was added. In particular, the "diavlos" was equivalent to two stades, that is 384.54 meters. Because the runner covered twice the length of the track, they used to start from the finishing line of the "stadion" race so that the finish would be at the same point for both events. The first winner of the "diavlos" event was Ipinos from Pisa.

In 720 B.C., in the 15th Olympiad another foot-race, the "dolichos", was introduced. The dolichos was defined as equivalent to 24 stades (4,614.48 meters). The first winner was the Spartan Akanthos.

In the Olympiad of 708 B.C., two more events are introduced, wrestling and "pentathlon". The latter combined five events, the stadion, wrestling, javelin and discus throwing and the long jump.

A statue in the Vatican.

In 688 B.C. there is for the first time reference to the event of boxing. The winner to the boxing event was the famous Onomastos from Smyrni.

In 680 B.C., the tethrippon (four-horse chariot race) was introduced.

In 648 B.C., the Pankration, a combination of boxing and wrestling was introduced. This constituted one of the most demanding and dangerous events and, as a result, there were very few entrants.

In 520 B.C. the race in armor was introduced. In this event the athletes ran carrrying their defensive panoply.

Later they carried only their shields. The first winner of this race was Damaretos of Gortynia.

In 632 B.C., during the 37th Olympiad boys' foot-race and wrestling were introduced. More specifically the boys had to cover one half of the length of the track, that is approximately 50 meters. The young boy Damiskos of Messenia won the boys' foot-race in the 103rd Olympiad (368 B.C.) at the age of twelve.

From the 7th century B.C. onwards Chariot races used to take place in the Hippodrome. As a rule the equestrian competitions involved three races: The tethrippon (four-horse chariot race). The synoris (two-horse chariot race) adn the "keles", a race for horses with a rider.

Finally, the Marathon was introduced in order to commemorate the Messenger Pheidippides who ran the distance from Marathon to Athens to announce the Greek

A resting discus thrower, statue in the Vatican.

The discus thrower ot Myron.

Race-in-armor athletes depicted on an ancient vase.

victory over the Persians at the battle of Marathon. The Marathon race coverd 42,195 meters.

With the passage of time the program of the Olympics became richer as more and more events were included and the number of athletes wishing to participate rose.

Other events were the following:

The **Jump,** according to which the competitors were required to hurl their bodies and cover the maximum possible distance. Jumping was performed in a rectangular pit, usually 50 feet long, dug out and covered with soft soil.

The softness of the soil served two functions. First, it prevented the athletes from hurting themselves, and, second, it helped distinguish and, subsequently, measure the performance of each athlete.

Some athletes, like the famous Phayllos of Kroton were

believed to have managed to jump longer than the pit and reach the hard soil.

The **Discus,** which was originally made of stone, and later of metal. The discus is discribed by the historian Loukianos as very heavy. From archeological discoveries we have found that the discus ranged from 17 to 30 centimeters in diameter, it had a weight of about 2 kilos and it was lens-shaped.

The **Javelin** was a hollow wooden pole with a pointed iron end. At the other end of the javelin there was attached a thong, a strip of leather that formed a loop in order to facilitate a more powerful throw of the javelin.

The program of the Olympic Games became more systematic in 472 B.C. and was maintained in this form until the second century A.D.

The following comments are in order here: Chariot Races:

The equestrian events used to take place on the third day of the Olympic Games. The first equestrian event was the chariot races, which were held in the hippodrome. In various points of the hippodrome there were statues and altars dedicated to Poseidon Hippios, Hera Hippia, Mars Hippios, Athena Hippia, etc.

The chariot races were probably the most spectacular of the Olympic events. The race course attracted the richest and most powerful Greeks who participated in the races either personally or by representative.

During the chariot races every charioteer tried to position himself in the inside of the hippodrome so as to shorten the distance to be coverd. Pretty often, collisions and other, occasionally fatal, accidents occured.

Such accidents usually involved inexpert charioteers.

Pugilist, statue in the Museum of Dresde.

The various types of Chariot races were introduced in the Olympic Games in the following chronological order:

The **tethrippon** (four-horse chariot) was the first chariot race that was ever held in the Olympics. The Theban Pagondas is mentioned as the first tethrippon winner in Olympic history.

The **apene,** a chariot pulled by two mules, was introduced in the 70th Olympiad. The first such race was won by the Thessalian Thersios.

The **synoris,** a chariot pulled by a pair of horses, was first introduced during the 93rd Olympiad. Evagoras of Elis is known to have won the first synoris race.

The **tethrippon for foals** was introduced in the 99th Olympiad. It was won by Sybariades of Sparta.

The **synoris for foals** was introduced in the 128th Olympiad, and was won by a woman, Belestiche of Madedonia. It should be noted here that the right of women to patricipate in the chariot races was first instituted during the 90th Olympiad.

The first woman ever to win a chariot race was Kyniska, the daughter of the Spartan king Archidamos and sister of Agesilaos.

Running

The runners were divided into groups. This was inevitable since the number of the participants was larger than the number of the positions provided for runners in the stadium.

The runner who would record the great achievement of winning in three running events the **stadion,** the **diaulos** and the rase in armor, was honorably called **triastes.** Such athletes were Leonidas of Rhodes (164 B.C. — 152 B.C.), Hekatomnos of Miletos (72 B.C.), Polites of Keramos, and others.

The runners originally used to wear a kind of loin-cloth, but in later times they ran naked. According to tradition, the first runner to take off his cloth was Orsippos of Megara.

Running was the most popular athletic event in the ancient times. In addition, it appears to have had much

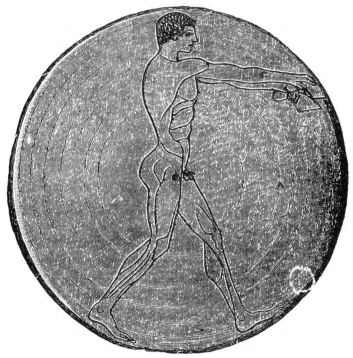

Scene of a jumper engraved on a copper discus from Aigina. The athlete holds jumping-weights (Museum of Berlin).

practical importance as well. It should be mentioned in this context that it was Pheidippides the Messenger that the Athenians sent to Sparta to call for reinforcements in the Greek war against the Persians. This shows that a runner was considered preferable to other means of transport like the horse or the boat. Also, we should mention here Euchidas who ran the distance from Plataia to Delphi and returned on the same day to die shortly after his arrival, probably as a result of exhaustion.

Another Boeotian athlete, Lasthenis, managed to beat a horse in a running cempetition from Koroneia to Thebes.

The kretans and the Arcadians appear to have been the best **dolichos** runners. They often served as heralds and messengers and trained systematically to improve their performance in long distance travel on foot.

Another running event was the torch-race, **lampadedromia** in Greek. It was basically a religious ceremony. It took place at night. An interesting variation was the torch-race on horseback. The torch-bearers held, a torch in their hand.

Wrestling

Wrestling was the second event in the Olympic Games. Each competitor drew a lot from a helmet. On the lot was written a letter designating his opponent. The winners of each wrestling contest was then again divided in pairs and so on until there remained only the two finalists.

According to plutarch, wrestling was the most skillful and cunning athletic competition. This description was consistent with the Olympic spirit of the time, which allowed the competitor to use various wrestling techniques and tricks.

Such things as strangle-holds, dislocating of the

opponent's fingers, gripping the opponent's body with the legs, seizing the opponent from behind, etc., were absolutely permissible.

Wrestling was very familiar throughout the antiquity. According to mythology, Zeus wrestled with Kronos, Aias with Odysseus in the contests honoring the dead Patroclos, and Odysseus with Philomeides on the island of Lesbos.

There were two forms of wrestling: "upright" wrestling (in Greek, **orthia pale, orthopale,** or **stadaia pale**) and "rolling" or "ground" wrestling (alindesis or kylisis, or kato pale). In the firts form of wrestling, victor was proclaimed the wrestler who managed to throw his opponent to the ground three times. In the second, the fight continued until one of the wrestlers conceded defeat and quit.

The art of wrestling was believed to have been invented by Theseus.

The qualities required of a good wrestler were in summary the following: skill, scientific method, swiftness, sharp reflexes, and acute ability to discern and, if possible, predict the opponent's next move.

One of the most famous wrestlers in ancient Greece was Milon of Kroton, son of Diotimos, whose physical strength became a legend. One of the best known wrestlers that Milon managed to beat, was Tithormos. Also, Kratinos, o boy from Aigeira in Achaia was highly admired in Olympia for his wrestling ability. As a result he was allowed to erect a statue of himself and of his teacher.

The Pentathlon

Of all contests, the pentathlon was cosidered to be the most honorable and noble. It was highly respected by the ancient Greeks because it was supposed to test accurately the physical condition, strength and courage of the athletes. We can therefore say that the pentathlon winners were justly regarded as the best of men, since they had to compete in five consecutive events.

Only men were allowed to take part in the pentathlon. However, duting the 35th Olympiad young boys were also granted permission to compete. During this Olympiad a boy from Sparta, Eutichidas, won the pentathlon event. Subsequently, the Eleans decided that no boys would be allowed to compete in the pentathlon event in the Olympic Games.

The pentathlon victor who managed to win all five events was proclaimed **pentathlos.** Understandably, this was very rare.

The Pankration

Herakles was by and large a pankratiast, while Theseus is considered to be the founder of this event that combined wrestling and boxing. This heavy and tremendously demanding event was first introduced in the Games during the 23rd Olympiad, that is in 648 B.C. To succeed in the Pankration event an athlete had to be swift, skillful, and strong.

Among the most famous pankratiasts was Sokrates of Sikyon who could twist the arms of his opponents so violently that they withdrew immediately.

However the best known pankratiast was Polydamas of Skotoussa in Thessaly, whose whole life was a ceaseless sequence of physical achievements. One event, the killing of a strong, big lion by Polydamas' bare hands, made Polydamas almost the equal of the legendary Herakles. On another occasion Polydamas managed to bring to a halt a speeding chariot, simply by holding the rear of the chariot with one hand. Finally we should mention here the case of Arrichion of Phigaleia in Arcadia, who became immortal in Olympic history. In particular, in a desperate effort to got rid of his opponent's deadly grip, he gathered his remaining strength and broke his opponent's ankle. His opponent, raised his hand in admission of defeat, while at the same moment Arrichion passed away. As a result, the dead Arrichion was proclaimed Olympic victor, since his opponent had quit the fight.

The pankration was later dropped from the program of the Olympics becuase it was thought to be barbarous and inhuman.

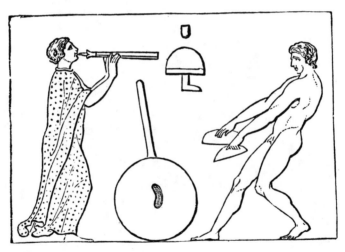

Jumper holding weights, ancient vase.

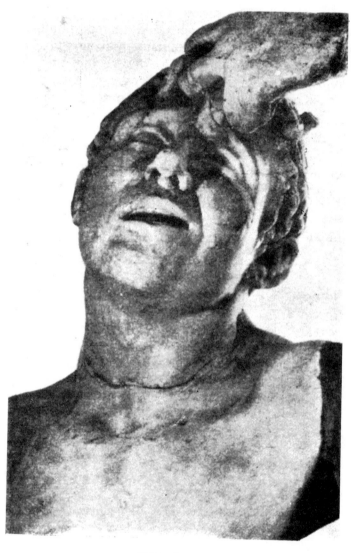

Pankratiast.

Boxing

Boxing was one of most cunning and ancient sports. The boxers, originally, wrapped **himantes** that is straps of soft ox-hide round their hands in order to strengthen their wrists and steady their fingers. Later, in order to make the blows effective, they added straps of harder leather around the knuckles of the fingers.

There is still no concrete historical evidence as to the exact form of the area in which the contest was held. Further, the boxing match lasted until one of the opponents conceded defeat. Also, the modern classification of the boxers (heavy weight, light weight etc) was not known to the ancient Greeks.

Despite the prevailing at the time rules of boxing, injuries were frequently bad and occasionally fatal. For example, Kleomedes of Astypalaia, in 496 B.C., killed his opponent Inikos of Epidaurus during their boxing contest. Also Diognetos of Krete was held responsible for the death of his opponent, a Herakles. As a conequence, Diognetos was refused to be crowned victor and, in addition, was expelled from Olympia.

Some of the most famous boxers of mythology were Theseus and Herakles. The latter was also credited with the introduction of the boxing contest.

From the ancient Greeks we should mention here Milon of Kroton, an Olympic victor who was also known to have killed a cow with a blow; Theagenes of Thasos who won in various athletic contests 1400 prizes; (it should be mentioned here that Theagenes, while he was still a boy, stole a heavy statue of a god and, after being arrested, escaped a death sentence on account of his young age). Diagoras of Rhodes was proclaimed Olympic victor for his boxing victories.

Head of a boxer.

The last of the known Olympic victors in boxing appears to have been the Armenian boxer Artavasdos who won the boxing contest in 385 B.C.

In order to improve the athletic spirit, the Hellanodikai (Judges) decided at some stage in Olympic history to reward most those boxers who managed to win without causing severe injuries to their opponents. Conversely, the judges often refused to declare victors those boxers who intentionally or even as a result of carelessness caused serious damage to their opponents.

Jumping

Jumping, like running, was one of the best known and most popular sports in ancient Greece. In the eighth raspody of Homer's Odyssey, jumping appears to be part of the Phaiakian games.

In the Olympic games, jumping was introduced during the 18th Olympiad, that is in 708 B.C. The execution of this event is described below.

Jumping was performed in the **skamma.** This was a 50 — foot rectangular pit, dug out and filled with soft soil. Before, an athlete jumped, the soil was flattened in order to erase the marks of the previous jumper.

According to the rules of jumping, each competitor, before jumping, had to step on the **bater** a fixed point on one side of the rectangular pit. The **bater** was also the point from which the length of the jump was measured. So the jump of each athlete was the distance from the bater to the point where his feet hit the soft soil.

While jumping, the athletes held jumping weights called **halteres.** These **halteres,** made of iron, helped the jumpers balance their bodies and improve their performance.

During the performance of the jumping event, flutists (**avleteres** in Greek) played their instruments, according to the historian Pausanias.

There appear to have been three types of jump.

a) Long jump with and without a run up.

b) High jump and long jump with and without a run up.

c) Deep jump.

The latter jump was performed over a properly constructed ditch.

Jumping was considered to be the most difficult of the pentathlon events and, therefore, was specially admired by the ancient Greeks.

Among the famous jumpers of the antiquity we should mention the following.

The jumper Lampis who is known to have been the first Olympic victor in jumping.

Hysmon of Elis who is referred to in historical sources as a great athlete and jumper. Hysmon is said to have suffered from rheumatisms since his childhood and took up various sports in order to improve his physical condition. As a result of this training, not only did he rid himself of his handicap but also turned out to become and excellent athlete, achieving victories in Nemea and Olympia. A statue of himself holding jumping weights is still preserved in the sacred Altis of Olympia.

Discus

The discus throwing event had a long tradition in the Greek world. The earliest appearance of this sport is connected with Homer's Iliad. In this epic work, that we find a discus throwing competition in the funerary games organized by Achilles in honor of his dead friend Patroklos. In this competition participated Aias of Telamon, Leonteas,

Polypoites and Epeios. Polypoites won the competition and appears to have been the first discus victor in recorded history.

From Homer's description of the event we deduce that the discus was one of the oldest sports.

In Greek mythology, the discus is bound up with accidents and killings. In particular, Apollo killed Hyakinthos with a discus because of jealousy, Perseus inintentionally killed his grandfather Akrisios who was father of Danae and king of Argos, in a tragic accident that happened in Larisa. Phokos killed with a discus his brother Telamon.

The discus was introduced in the Games during the 18th Olympiad. The first Olympic victor of this event was Lampis.

During the Homeric times as well as initially in Olympia, the discus was made of stone, because iron was relatively rare. In Homer, the iron discus was called **Solos**. Later, the discus was made of bronze, copper and lead. The discus used in ancient Greece resembled its modern counterpart. In particular, the discus was round with two convex curves in section and a large circumference. On the average, the discus had a diameter of 30 centimeters and weighed 2 kilos. However, archeologists have discovered a discus of 34 centimeters in diameter. According to the incription on this discus, Poplios Asklepiades had dedicated the discus to Zeus, as a thanksgiving for his victory in the pentathlon event, in 241 B.C. Further, an oval shaped stone has been discovered, 143.5 kilos, 33 cm high, 68 cm long, and 38 cm. wide. According to a relevant inscription an athlete named Bybon, a son of Pholas, succeeded in raising this stone high, above his head, with one hand.

The distance covered by the discus from the point it

was thrown to the point it landed was called "discoura". The performance of each discus-thrower was marked with a small peg and measured with rods.

Some of the most famous discus-throwers were the Olympic victor Euryvotas and Hysmosn of Elis that we also mentioned in the jumping event.

Javelin

In the Homeric times, the javelin was a most important military exercise and as such it was highly respected. As an athletic event was also considered to be useful, difficult and occasionally accident-prone.

The heroes and warriors of the antiquity honored and loved the javelin and were expert in handling it.

Javelin thrower, ancient copper discus.

The javelin was a hollow wooden pole with a pointed iron end. In length it ranged from 1.85 to 2.40 meters. It was about 3 cm thick.

The competitors, depending on the particular version of the javelin, threw the javelin, either standing upright, or running, or from a kneeling position. The javelin was thrown from a specified point. Apart from the event of throwing the javelin for distance, there was also the event of target javelin. The latter was usually performed from horseback or from chariots.

Throwing the javelin at a target from horseback was mostly a military exersice and therefore was not practiced in the gymnasiums.

However, it was highly admired among the ancient Greeks.

Originally, the javelin was considered to be a barbaric weapon and, of all the Greeks, only the Aitoloi used it. According to the ancient commentator Euripides, the Aitoloi were most expert javelin-throwers.

In the mythical times, the victor of the javelin event in the competition organized by Herakles was an athlete named Phrastor.

The javelin as an event of the official Olympic program was introduced during the 18th Olympiad as one of the five events cosntituting the Pentathlon.

The javelin training of the ancient Greeks was related to its usefulness in war and hunting.

4.7. Intellectual Games

In Olympia, apart from competition that tested physical strength, there were also held games that tested the strength of the intellect. Writers, historians, sophists, poets, used to go the Olympic Games to read their works or put forward their ideas.

Herodotos, credited as the father of history, read the first part of his monumental work during the 81st Olympiad, at the age of 28.

The eminent sophists Hippias and Gorgias taught the

gathered crowds. The latter, delivered his Olympic speech in the 88th Olympiad.

During the 91st Olympiad, in 416 B.C., the tragic poet Xenokles competed against the legendary Euripides.

Lysias and Isokrates read their writings in the Olympic gatherings and impressed the people. Also, powerful but not very gifted people attempted to gain Olympic glory and to this end read their poems and other works in the Olympic gatherings, only to be booed and jeered by the crowds. This was, for example, the case of Dionysios, the wealthy tyrant of Syracuse, who repeatedly sent magnificient missions to Olympia including chariots to compete in the races and orators to read his poems.

Hoever, his expectations of glorious victories suffered such a debacle that the enraged Dionysios eventually had his charioteers beheaded and his orators exiled.

Further, there were held competitions of works of art and artistic exhibitions. For instance, Aetion presented a painting of his that illustrated the wedding of Alexander the Great.

4.8. Trumpeters' and Heralds' competitions

The trumpeters' and heralds' competitions were somewhat peculiar. These events were first introduced in Olympia in 396 B.C. and used to take place during the first day of the Olympic Games.

The origin of these competitions was due to the fact that there were many able trumpeters and heralds who wanted eagerly to play the privileged role of announcing the athletic events and the Olympic victors, or of blowing the trumpet. As loudspeakers were inexistent at that time, the heralds were required to have very loud and clear voices in order to be heard all over the stadium. The best solution to the problem of oversupply of competent heralds and trumpeters turned out to be the establishment of trumpeters' and heralds' competitions.

Archias of Sicily is referred as one of the most prominent herald of all times. He won the herald's competition in three consecutive Olympiads that took place in the middle of the fourth century B.C. In a word, Archias was unbeatable.

As far as the trumpeters' competitions are concerned, winner was proclaimed the trumpeter whose trumpet could be heard as far away as possible. For example, a famous trumpeter, Epitades, could be heard to a distance of over six miles. However, Herodoros seems to have been the most famous trumpeter in the antiquity.

Herodoros was a huge man, extremely tall, a legenderay eater and drinker. He used to sleep on a bear's skin and wore a lion's skin. He would eat six **choinikes** of bread (approximately six kilograms), twenty **litrai** of meat, and drink two **choai** of wine. He won the trumpeter's competition in almost a dozen Olympiads. He used to blow the trumpet, or occasionally two trumpets, so forcibly that he inspired and encouraged the crowds.

In this context of our presentation, it should be of interest to mention a woman trumpeter, Aglais, a tall woman that had first been admired for her ability to blow the trumpet in Alexandria of Egypt, where she used to be a trumpeter in the long processions.

4.9. Music contests

As the music was considered by the ancient Greeks to improve the spirit and revitalize the body, it was inextricably bound up with the upbringing of the young and important part of all education. In the music competitions, the participants competed either individually or in groups, and either sang or played musical instruments. In our opinion the reintroduction of some form of musical competitions in the Olympic Games, would be a most useful development in the modern version of the Games.

4.10. The rights of the athletes

Thirty days before the inauguration of the Olympiad, the judges (Hellanodikai) closed the list of the athletes that were to take part in the Games.

There followed qualifying contests which led to the elimination of those athletes that were judged as unsuitable.

After the judges proclaimed the winner of each Olympic event, they gave him a palm branch. At the end of each Olympiad, the judges wrote on an official document the names of the Olympic victors.

The decisions of the Hellanodikai were final and irrevorable. All Greeks trusted the sincerity, judgement, and impartiality of the Hellanodikai. However, if an athlete thought that he had been discriminated against, he could resort to the House of the Elians. If the House thought that the athlete was right, it could impose sanctions on the judges. Nevertheless, the House could not reverse the judges' decisions.

4.11. Program of the Olympic Games

The program of the Olympic Games included all ceremonies and events. Initially, the Games lasted for one day, but later, that Is from 468 B.C., the duration of tho Games became five days. The first day was dedicated, among other things, to the registration of the athletes and to the draw of the positions of the athletes and the **Hellanodikai** in front of the statue of Zeus Horkios (Horkos is the Greek word for oath) at the **Bouleuterion** (Council House). It was during this first day of the Games that the leaders of the Eleans offered the hetacomb to Zeus, the great deity of Olympia. Then, the ceremony went on with the offerings and sacrifices by representatives of the various cities in front of the altar of Zeus. The representatives were called **theoroi.** Finally, the athletes sacrificed to Zeus. After the sacrifices, the athletes were led by the **Hellanodikai** in front of the above mentioned statue of Zeus Horkios. The god has his arms raised and holds thunderbolts in his hands. First took the official oath the Hellanodikai, who swear that they would judge the athletes impartially. Then the trainers swore that they had scrupulously trained the athletes. Finally, the athletes swore that they had trained diligently, that they were free Greek citizens, that they had never been found guilty of murder, and that they would compete fairly and not pursue the victory by illegal means.

Also during the first day, a youth, whose father and mother were alive, cut from the ancient wild olive tree as many branches as there were contests to make the crowns for the victors. The youth used gold shears and this ceremony had a fistive character as the local authorities and the representatives from the various cities were present.

On this first day of the Olympiad, the heralds' and trumpeters' competitions were held. The winners were those whose voices of trumpets, respectively, carried farthest. They had the privilege to call out the names of the athletes and to blow the trumpet throughout the Games.

On the second day the boys' competitions took place. Also, during this day the equestrian competitions were held. The most spectacular of these competitions were undoubtedly the chariot races. It should be reminded here, that it was the owner of the horses, not the charioteer, who was declared victor. The chariots took their positions at the starting point and had to complete twelve circuits, that is fourteen kilometers (approximately).

During the morning of the third day the running events were held, while during the evening the wrestling, the boxing, and the pankration.

During the fourth day took place the race in armor and the pentathlon.

Finally, during the fifth and last day of the Games, the crowning ceremony of the victors was held.

4.11a. Qualifications for the participation in the Olympic Games

To be allowed to take part in the Games, an athlete should:
1. Be a citizen of Greece.
2. Not have ever been convicted of murder or sacrilege.
3. Be a free man, not a slave.
4. Have trained for a period of at least ten months in a

proper athletic track and for at least thirty days in Olympia under the supervision of Hellanodikai.

Also excluded from the Games was anyone who had shown disrespect to a god.

4.12. Prizes awarded to the Olympic victors

The Olympic victors were initially given cash prizes and other valuable objects and gifts. However, from 748 B.C., the only prize awarded for victory at Olympia was the **kotinos,** a crown made of branches of wild olive. According to a tradition, the wild olive tree from which the branches were cut, had been planted in front of the temple of Zeus by Hercules. It is also said that it was Iphitos who established the crown of wild olive as the Olympic prize. It should be clear that the institution of the olive crown as the sole award given to the Olympic victors, removed the concept of material profit from the Games and placed the competition for Olympic distinction in the sphere of pure glory, honor, and respect.

4.13. The award of the prizes

The final day of the Games was dedicated to the award of the prizes. The mood that prevailed was terribly jovial. The victors were coming down the stadium wearing ribbons around their foreheads and holding the palm-branches that they had been given immediately after their victories. The crowds of spectators followed them, overcome with joy, applauding, clapping, lifting winners of their shoulders, throwing flowers on the winners, waving palm-branches. The procession was led by the Hellanodikai who finally took up their positions in front of the temple of Zeus. The crowns were placed on the gold and ivory table that had been constructed by the sculptor Kolotos. The head of the Hellanodikai pronounced the name of the first victor, who was always the victor of the **stadion** race. This athlete had the unique honor of giving his name to the Olympiad. The herald called the name of the athlete who was then crowned with the sacred **kotinos** and proclaimed **Olympionikes,** that is Olympic victor. Immediately afterwards the herald pronounced the name of the victor, his father's name, and his birthplace.

Then, the friends and fellow-country men of the crowned victor rushed up, lifted him on their shoulders and carried him round among the joyful spectators. These scenes were repeated for each Olympic victor.

After their crowning ceremony, the victors followed by the Hellanodikai and the crowds moved solemnly towards the altars where they offered thanksgiving sacrifices to the gods.

The near-immortality which the Olympic fame ensured the victors was so highly valued by the ancient Greeks that there have been recorded a few cases in which a victor's father died of a heart attack caused by the intense emotion during the crowning of his son. This was the case of Cheilon the Wise who died during the 56th Olympiad while watching the crowning ceremony of his son.

At mid-day, the Eleans gave a banquet for the winners of all contests in the Prytaneion. During the banquet, the **epinician hymns** were recited. These were victory odes which the victors or their cities commissioned poets to write for them. Until late at night, the valley of Olympia echoed with songs, hymns, paeans, wishes and congratulations.

The following day, it was customary for the Olympic victors to give a banquet for the **Hellanodikai,** their fellow-countrymen, and, occasionaly, some of the **theoroi.** These banquets were very expensive. As a result the largerst part or the whole of the cost was undertaken by the victors' cities. For, example, it is known that the city of Athens and its allies covered the huge cost of a banquet given by Alkiviades.

4.14. The crowning of the victors

The most touching moment for every athlete was that during which his long period of effort and training was rewarded by the crown of Olympic victory. No material or intangible reward could compare with the wild olive crown of the Olympics. Diagoras of Rhodes, himself an Olympic victor, had the unique happiness to see in 448 B.C. his two sons win in Olympia, Damagetos in the Pankration and Akousilaos in Boxing. Just after their crowning, the two victors lifted their old father on their shoulders and carried him round the stadium. A Spartan shouted at Diagoras: "Now you may happilly die Diagoras. You have lived up to the highest possible glory. You have become a near-god". Shortly afterwards, Diagoras died of a heart attack caused, apparently, by excessive emotion, pleasure, and happiness.

Diagoras, a former Olympic victor, carried on the shoulders of his sons, shortly after their Olympic victories.

4.15. Olympic Victors

Eight hundred and fifty are the Olympic victors whose names are preserved, carved on marble stones. Below we present a selection of the famous and impressive Olympic winners.

Runners

The Spartan Ladas won the **dolichos** in 440 B.C. However, immediately after his victory, Ladas got ill and died while he was being carried to Sparta where he was buried.

Argeus or **Aigeus** won the **dolichos** in 328 B.C. Then, without waiting to be crowned, he set off and ran all day to reach Argos in the evening of the same day and announce his Olympic victory. It should be noted that the distance from Olympia to Argos is 90 Kilometers, that is more than twice the distance of the Marathon.

Chionis of Sparta won the **stadion** race four times and the **diaulos** three times.

Dandis of Argos won the **discus** in 476 B.C. and the **stadion** race in 472 B.C. Also, he was declared **periodonikes** because he had won victories in all four great Panhellenic competitions, that is in the Pythian, Nemean, Isthmian and Olympic Games of the same period.

Damischos of Messinia, won the boys' foot-race at the age of twelve. Also, he won the pentathlon in the Nemean and Pythian Games.

Polymestor of Miletos who according to Philostratos was so fast that one day he chased a hare and caught it alive.

Wrestlers

Milon of Kroton, son of Diotimos first won at Olympia in the boys' wrestling, in 540 B.C. He was also proclaimed victor another five times in the men's wrestling at Olympia, six times in the Pythian, nine in the Nemean and ten in the Isthmian Games.

Neverthless, Milon never managed to defeat Titormos, a shepherd from Aitolia.

Straton or **Stratonikos** of Alexandria, who was proclaimed **periodonikes** and also, in 68 B.C. **paradoxonikes,** that is he managed the very difficult feat to win the wrestling and the pankration on the same day in an Olympiad. When he moved to Aigion, the city authorities built a special training area for him.

Taurosthenes of Aigina, won in the wrestling in 444 B.C. and according to legend, a pigeon carried the news from Olympia to Aigina on the same day after flying a distance of approximately 160 kilometers.

Demokrates of Tenedos whose statue was erected in the Altis of Olympia.

Amesinas of Barka who used to train by wrestling with a bull.

Boxers

Diagoras of Rhodes, son of Damagetos, appears to have been the most famous boxer of ancient Greece. He won twice at Olympia, twice in Nemea, four times at the Isthmian Games and an unknown number of times in the Pythian Games. He was idolized by Pindar in his 9th ode.

Pythagoras of Samos (not the philosopher), who went to Olympia to participate in the boys' contest but was not allowed to do so and fought in the men's boxing, defeating all his opponents.

Glaukos of Karystos, son of Demylos, won in the boys' boxing in 480 B.C., later became a renowned boxer and was proclaimed **periodonikes** after winning at Olympia, at the Pythian, at the Nemean and at the Isthmian games. He was buried by the Karystians in a little island that was given his name.

Theagenes of Thassos, probably the most famous of all boxers, won from twelve hundred to fourteen hundred boxing victories and was proclaimed twice **periodonikes.**

Pankratiasts

Kallias of Athens, son of Didymos, won in 472 B.C., during a prankration fight that lasted until late at night. He won another twelve times. In Olympia, a huge statue o Kallias was erected, a masterpiece made of copper by the famous artist Mikon of Athens.

Phrynon of Athens won in 636 B.C. and later became a general of the Athenian army. He was killed by Pittakos, one of the renowned Seven Wise Men, during the war of the Athenians against the island of Mytilene.

Ephoudion of Mainalon, Arcadia, won at an old age his much younger Askondas, in 464 B.C.

Polydamas of Scotoussa (an ancient city lying between Larissa and Pharsala), won in 408 B.C. His life was full of incredible achievements. For example, he killed a strong, wild, big lion unarmed; he brought to a halt a chariot that was passing by at great speed. Polydamas' statue is still partly preserved in the Museum of Olympia.

Although some of the feats attributed to various athletes seem too impressive to have been true, there is much historical evidence to testify that they belong to the sphere of reality, not of fiction.

Pentathletes

The most famous pentathlon victors appear to have been the following four:

Gorgos of Messine, Gorgos of Elis, Krakanos or Grakanos of Sikyon, and Ainitos.

Three were the most ancient statues representing Olympic victors at Olympia. That of Eutelidas of Sparta, victor in the boys' wrestling and pentathlon, in 628 B.C., that of Praxidamas of Aigina, victor in the boxing in 544 B.C. His statue was made of wood from cypress-tree; and that of Rexibios of Opus, victor in the pankration in 536 B.C. This statue was made of wood from fig-tree.

4.16. The return home of the Olympic victors The meaning of their victory

The honors conferred on the Olympic victors were most distinctive. The victory meant great glory both for the athlete and for his native city.

The return home of the Olympic victors and their entry into the city was done in a very festive way. The victor was given a delirious welcome. Standing upright in a magnificient four-horse chariot, he entered the city but not through the gates. Part of the city's walls was brought down specially for the victor's entry. The meaning behind this custom was that a city that had produced such a man no longer needed the protective shield of the walls. The triumphal entry into the city was followed by a festive procession of the victor followed by the city authorities and virtually the whole people. The assembled crowds showered him with flowers. The Olympic victor, passing through the central city area, went to the sanctuary of the patron deity of the city to dedicate his crown and offer thanksgiving sacrifices. Then he went to the Prytaneion of his city and attended the great celebratory banquet that was given by the city in order to honor further the victor and to which occasionally the whole city was invited.

It is said that Euxenetos of Sicily, after winning a number of Olympic victories, entered festively his city followed by a procession of five hundred chariots pulled by white horses.

The privileges enjoyed by the Olympic victors were exceptional and varied from city to city. For example, they had a special seat at the public games and sometimes were appointed Hellanodikai. Also, they had seats of honor at the theater, at religious festivities, and at the **agora.** Occasionally, they were exempted from paying taxes. In Sparta, the Olympic victor enjioyed the supreme privilege of fighthing in war at the side of the king.

The honors enjoyed by the victors were often of a material character. For example, many cities granted their Olympic victors annual salaries. In Athens, Solon instituted a law according to which each Olympic victor would be offered five hundred drachmas, while each victor in the Inthmian Games would get a hundred drachmas.

Also, every city, to honor its victor, gave him the right to set up a statue of himself and to erect it in such a place of the city that it could be most immediately seen by the passers by. Often, the statues were built at public expense.

To perpetuate his name, an Olympic victor had the right to erect a statue of himself in the sacred Altis at Olympia. An inscription accompanying the statue included the name of the victor and the athletic event in which he had won.

It should be noted at this point that the material benefits and other privileges conferred on the Olympic victors were greatly inferior to the glory and virtual immortality that the title of Olympic victor ensured an athlete. Also, the reader should be reminded at this point that the most highly regarded contest was that of running and thus the winner of the **stadion** race gave his name to the respective Olympiad.

The privileges of the Olympic victors were maintained more or less intact until the era of emperor Trianos who issued an edict according to which Olympic victors would be given only a sum of money that was called **Opsonia**. Still later, under Diocletian and Maximian, the successors of Trianos, the privileges were reduced to a minimum and gradually disappeared to the point that during the last few Olympiads, Olympic victors were not even allowed to carve their names on stones at Olympia.

4.17. The spectators — The exclusion of women

Spectators of varied backgrounds and countries used to arrive in Olympia to follow the Games. For example, the renowned philosopher Socrates used to go on foot to

Olympia, while Thales of Miletos was once seen, at the age of eighty, in ill health, among the spectators.

As it has already been mentioned elsewhere, the Eleans did not allow women to watch the Games. The rationale behind this decision is not absolutely clear. According to one view, the prohibition was meant to protect women against the very strong summer heat, although one suspects that if this were the case, women could best be left to decide for themselves. Another view has it that the exclusion of women was dictated by the prevailing morals of the time, since the athletes competed maked. The spectacle, however, was watched by one woman only, the priestess of the godess Demeter Chamyne.

She used to be seated on the altar of Mother Earth, inside the stadium, across the seats of the senior Hellanodikai, admiring the physical strength of the athletes. For example, Herodes Atticus, succeeding in having his wife Regilla chosen priestess of Demeter Chamyne by the Eleans. As a result, she could attend the Games.

The penalty for wome who chalenged the law concerning the exclusion of women was the ultimate punishment, death. Specifically, any woman who entered the stadium on the days the Games were held, would be thrown by the Eleans from the high precipitous cliffs of mount Typaion, which lay between Olympia and Skylon, on the left bank of the river Alhpeios.

The only woman that appears to have infringed this law and escaped death, was kallipateira, the daughter of Diagoras of Rhodes, the famous boxer and Olympic victor, and a sister of three excellent athletes and Olympic victors, Damagetos, Akousilaos, and Dorieus. After her husband's death, Kallipateira undertook to train her son Peisidoros for the Olympics. Then, she accompanied him to Olympia to participate in the Games and she entered the stadium perfectly disguised as a male trainer. She remained unnoticed in the special trainers' enclosure. However, when Peisidoros won his contest, she jumped over the fence and rushed to embrace him, but in doing so she lost her clothes.

The astonished Hellanodikai, however, accepted her explanation that as six male members of her family were Olympic victors she should have been allowed to watch the Games, and let her go free. From another point of view, the above incident led to the institution of a law according to which not only all athletes but also the trainers were required to be naked at the Games.

Not withstanding the above prohibition, there were cases in which a woman was proclaimed Olympic victor. This happened in the equestrian events, in which it was to the owner of the chariot or horse and not to the charioteer or rider that went the title of Olympic victor. Thus, Kyniska the daughter of Archidamos, king of Sparta, is referred to as the first woman Olympic victor, as she owned the victorious four-horse chariot in the relevant contest in 392 B.C. Ironically, therefore, women could become Olympic victors in the equestrian events although they were not permitted to watch the events!

4.18. The Olympiad

"Olympiad" was called the time period that intervened between two successive Olympic Games. The first Olympiad during which began the recording of the Olympic victors was that of 776 B.C.

In particular, the first victor ever to be recorded was the

Elean Koroibos. With the passage of time, the Olympiads constituted a stable basis for the ancient Greek dating system and gradually replaced the various local dating systems that had been prevalent in Athens, Sparta e.t.c.

The first historian who used the Olympiads as a universal dating system was Timotheos of Sicily. He was later followed by others like Diodoros of Sicily, Dionysios of Alikarnassos, Pausanias, and Aialianos.

5. RISE AND FALL OF THE OLYMPIC GAMES

5.1. Rise of the Games

The 4th century B.C. was characterized by intensive building activity that, as a result, transformed radically the outlook of the Altis. The Metroon, the temple of the Mother of Gods was built at the turn of the century, while the Phillipeion, the circular building south of the Prytaneion was also built during that century. It was during that century that the sanctuary was separated from the other buildings by a peribolos with gates in the west and the south side. Also, the south stoa was erected and formed the southern boundary of the sanctuary.

The 4th century is considered to be the brightest the period of the Olympic Games and coincides with the period during which occured the peak of the ancient Greek glory. During the 4th century the most famous Olympic victors were distinguished. Indicatively, we mention here Milon of Kroton, Diagoras of Rhodes, Polydamas of Scotoussa, Claukos of Karystos, Theagenes of Thasos, names to which we have referred in detail elsewhere in this book.

Kings from the distant Kyrene, tyrants from Sicily, princes from the powerful aristocracies of Korinth, Argos, and Thessaly, rich men from democratic cities, strove for distinction at Olympia, as if they felt that without an Olympic title something would be missing with their glory.

Kroisos, the immensely wealthy king of Lydia, brought to Olympia valuable gifts and priceless statues.

Alexander the Great, king of Macedonia, came to Olympia not to display his wealth but to declare his Greek origin and participate in the stadion race with the other athletes. He failed to distinguish himself in the contest and therefore missed the chance to be crowned Olympic victor.

The names of famous artists, such as Myron, Polykleitos, Phidias, Praxiteles, and Lyssipos are connected with some monumental sculptures that decorate the sacred buildings of the Altis.

Many philosophers, like Anaxagoras, Plato, and Aristotle, visited Olympia. Plato, in particular, created once sensation with his wisdom, while in Olympia icnognito.

According to tradition, the wise men Thales and Chilon died in Olympia while watching the Games. The sophists Prodikos, Gorgias, and Hippias delivered speeches there, and orators like Lysias and Isokrates addressed audiences on the subject of panhellenic unity. Lysias, in particular, recited his Olympic speech and reminded the Greeks that the Games' objective was to reconcile all the Greeks. Also, he urged the Olympic committee to exclude from participation the representatives sent by the tyrant of Sicily Dionysos and to organize a Greek expedition to free Sicily from Dionysios.

Herodotos, the great historian of the antiquity, became famous, after reading out to the crowds gathered in the temple of Zeus, a part of the history he had just finished writing. Among the audience was the young Thucydides who was later to become a great historian, best known for his account of the Peloponesiac war between Sparta and Athens.

Also, Olympia was visited by the astronomer Oinopides of Chios who left at Olympia a table made of copper, describing astrological calculations of that time. Finally, the great ancient painter Aetion, left at Olympia a painting representing the wedding of Alexander the Great and Roxani.

5.2. Decline of the Olympic Games

It is usually the case that during periods of cultural expansion like the one discribed in the previous section, the first signs of decadence begin to appear. Professional sport, as against pure athletics of the gymnasium, takes gradually over and the first cases of corruption among athletes and judges occur. During the 4th century B.C. several athletes are penalized for bribery. It is said that in 388 B.C., Eupolos of Thessaly bought off his competitor in order to win an Olympic boxing victory. The revenue from the fines was used to construct statues of Zeus, which as we will see later were called **Zanes.**

As a symptom of decadence can also be considered the incident during which a mob, under the influence of a speech by the orator Lysias, attacked and destroyed the tent of the tyrant Dionysios. This incident was clearly of political nature and should best be kept out of the Olympic Games.

As further sings of decadence we must also mention

the violations of the sacred truce that occasionally occurred within the Altis.

In 420 B.C., the Games took place under strict security measures because of the fear of an impending attack by the Spartans. Also, in 364 B.C. a bloody battle was given within the Altis, when the Eleans attempted to drive the Arcadians and Pisatans, who had organized the Games at that time, out of Olympia. Further, in 312 B.C., Telesphoros, a general of Antigonos, stormed Olympia and plundered the bursary of the sanctuary. A hundred years later, Philippos the Fifth, after subjecting Elis, settled for some time in Leonideon.

After Greece's subjection to Roman rule, the political decline of the country had unfortunate implications for the history of the sacred region of Olympia. Sulla, stripped the sanctuary of its pieces of art and later, in 80 B.C., celebrates the Olympic Games in Rome, as epinicean manifestation of the victory in the Mithridatic war. Calligula attempted unsuccessfully to have the gold and ivory statue of Zeus transported from Olympia to Rome. Nero transfers to Rome numerous pieces of art and in addition pronounces himself Olympic victor. However, some revival of the Games takes places during the reign of emperor Adrianos (117-138 A.D.) who ordered extensive restorations and extensions of the buildings at Olympia. Finally, in 267 B.C. Olympia underwent a raid by the Herouli.

Although the Olympic Games had degenerated long before they were officially abolished, their typical end came with a relevant edict by emperor Theodosius I, in A.D. 393. That was the year during which the 293rd and last Olympiad (or 291st according to some authors) was celebrated.

Two years later, the gold and ivory statue of Zeus was

transported to Constantinople and burnt. In 426 A.D., Theodosius II ordered that all statues in Olympia, including the temple of Zeus, should be destroyed as they were considered to be vestiges of paganism.

The above process of destruction was completed by two terrible earthquakes that occured in 522 and 551 A.D. and brought down the great constructions of the Olympic region. In the beginning of the 5th century a small Christian commune settled in the area where previously had existed the workshop of Pheidias, and built a byzantine church. Later, a slavic commune settled there, whose cemetery was found in the area of the Museum. During the Middle Ages came tremendous floods from the rivers Alpheios and Kladeos, while the collapses of stones and earth from the Kronion hill buried the whole of the sacred area of Olympia. Even the name "Olympia" was then forgotten. Until before the excavations, the area was locally known as Servia, or Serviana, and Antilalos.

5.3. Monuments and Buildings of Olympia
A. Within the area of the Altis
1. The Temple of Olympian Zeus

Of all buildings in the Altis the greatest was the temple of Zeus, the god of gods worshipped in ancient Greece and Rome. This temple was located in middle of the **peribolos** (enclosing wall). Within the temple stood the statue of the god. The temple was built by the famous Elean architect Libon, during the 5th century B.C. and was dedicated to Zeus by the Eleans as a thanksgiving for the victorious war against the Pisatans, the first inhabitants of ancient Olympia.

Reconstruction of the temple of Zeus.

The construction of the temple began in 470 B.C. and finished in 456 B.C. It is acknowledged that it constituted a model Doric temple. The sculptures on the pediments were made from marble and presented the chariot race between Oinomaos and Pelops, on the east side, while on the west side depicted the battle between the Lapiths and the Centaurs.

The twelve metopes were divided in the following way: six were above the entrance to the **pronaos** and six above the entrance of the **opisthodomos.** They depicted the twelve achievements of Hercules. This Doric temple was as large as the Parthenon of Athens.

Its dimensions were: length of 64.12 meters, width of 27.66 meters, and height of 20.25 meters. The columns had a height of 10.45 meters.

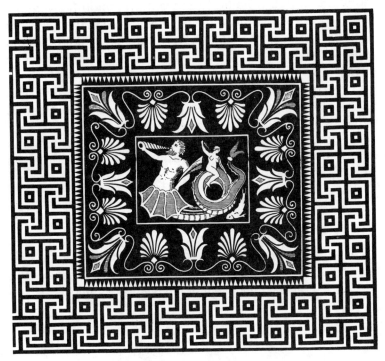

Mosaic work in the pronaos of the temple of Zeus.

The temple was divided into three sections.

a) The **pronaos** which was located on the east side and served as the main entrance of the temple.

b) The main temple which was separated from the **pronaos** with a series of columns.

c) The **opisthodomos** which was on the west side and had no access to the main temple but served as a storage area for the sacred objects of the temple.

A gold and ivory statue of Zeus, a masterpiece of the Athenian architect Pheidias, was set up inside the temple. The god was sitting on a throne. The statue had a height of 13 meters. The immense figure of the god held a gold and ivory Nike (victory) in his right hand and a sceptre with an angle in his left.

It was said that Pheidias had been inspired by some epic verses by Homer in his conception of this gigantic construction.

In order to describe the size of the statue which was seven times as big as the size of a normal male adult, the

The east pediment of the temple of Zeus.

The west pediment of the temple of Zeus.

ancient Greeks used to say: "If the god decided to rise from the throne, the roof of the temple would collapse".

Also, in expressing their admiration, people liked to exaggerate by saying: "Either Zeus visited the world and presented himself to Pheidias, or Pheidias payed the god a visit in heaven". Further, Epictetos said: "You must absolutely go to Olympia to see Zeus of Pheidias. It is a pity for anyone to die before seeing this masterpiece".

The interior of the temple of Zeus.

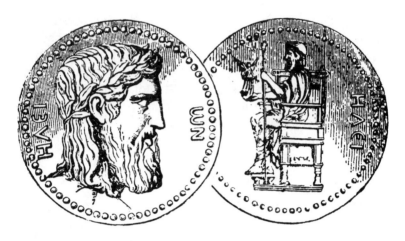

*Coin of the Eleans, illustrating the gold and ivory statue of Zeus,
which was a masterpiece made by Pheidias.*

Pausanias describes in every detail the artistic value of this masterpiece and gives a good idea of its mythical beuty. Dion Chrisostom, on the other hand, calls the statue "a happy picture" made with such realism of expression as to give the spectator the impression of a living thing.

Leukios Emilios Paul, who visited the temple in 167 B.C., was so amazed by the statue's magnificence that he thought he was seeing a living god.

According to a legend described by Pausanias, when Pheidias finished his work on the statue of Zeus, he asked the god for a sign expressing divine pleasure and approval. Shortly afterwards, the sought-for sign came in the form of a thunder. Further, according to another legend, Zues himself wrote on the base of the statue the statement: "Pheidias of Athens, a son of Harmides, made my statue".

Unfortunately, this greatly admired, respected and prai-

Zeus of Pheidias on a coin of the Eleans.

sed piece of art was not preserved and our impression of its art and value has been formed with the help of descriptions and judgements expressed by various ancient authors of which we shlould mention here the very detailed writings of Pausanias.

As it was mentioned earlier, Calligula once tried to have the statue transferred to Rome. In particular he planned to have Zeus' head replaced by another sculpture depicting his own (Calligula's) head. This plan, however, never materialized because of the technical difficulties involved in the transport venture. According to legend, the efforts of the Romans were repeatedly frustrated by the god's wrath which was expressed by unusually adverse weather conditions that hampered any attempt to remove the statue.

However, the statue was later to have an unfortunate end. This magnificent piece of art, the model of plasticity that withstood the attacks of men and time for a number of centuries, was eventually transported to Constantinople,

The temple of Zeus as it is today.

set afire and destroyed in 445 A.D. (or, according to others, in 475 A.D.).

Sometime between 150 A.D. and 170 A.D., the eminent sophist Lucianos saw the statue in a mutilated condition and chuckled: "Oh, Zeus, god of the gods, lord of the giants and titans; how can you tolerate to have your golden tentacles stolen? Why not use your mighty thunders?".

Ruins of the workshop of Pheidias which was turned into a Byzantive church.

A piece of art made by Pheidias. Under the Christian church of the 5th century B.C., in the sanctuary of Olympia, archaeological excavation brought to light the foundations of the workshop of the famous sculptor Pheidias. In this workshop Pheidias made the gold and ivory statue of Zeus. On the above depicted piece of art is engraved the statement: "I belong to Pheidias".

2. The Temple of Hera

This temple was built to honor the godess Hera, the Queen of the gods and wife of Zeus. According to mythology, Hera was the daughter of Kronos and Rea. This Doric temple, standing near the foot of Kronion, on the northwest side of the Altis was the oldest sacred building. The original temple, according to Pausanias, dates back to 1026 B.C. However, the temple of Hera took its final shape at the end of the 7th century B.C.

The temple is long and narrow. Its length is 50 meters and its width 18.75 meters. It has six columns along the

The temple of Hera as it is today.

width and sixteen along the legnth. The columns were initially made of wood, but were later replaced by stone ones. Most of the columns have been preserved until today. In the main temple there were various statues, of which the most famous were Hermes of Praxiteles, which is considered to be one of the brightest masterpieces of the autiquity and is still preserved, though not intact, in the Museum of ancient Olympia, and the statue of Zeus.

In the opisthodomos there were kept some important pieces of art, like the tray of Iphitos which contained the sacred armistice, the gold and ivory table on which the crowns for the Olympic victors were laid (the table was the work of the sculptor Kolotes), and the urn of Kypselos, tyrant of Corinth.

An aspect of the temple of Hera.

The Heraion.

A part of the temple of Hera in the Altis.

Hermes of Praxiteles (completed)

Hermes of Praxiteles as it is preserved today. Probably the most exquisite masterpiece of the antiquity. Hermes holds the infant god Dionysos.

The temple of Hera. The richest temple of ancient Olympia. Among other things, Hermes of Praxiteles was in this temple.

3. The Hippodameion

This was a temple devoted to the commemoration of Hippodameia, the mythical wife of Pelops. It lied to the north-east of the temple of Zeus, a short distance from the Bouleuterion. In the middle of the Hippodameion there was an altar. Once a year, women were allowed to enter the mosque and offer sacrifices to Hippothameia.

4. The Pelopeion

This shrine lied between the great temple of Zeus and the temple of Hera. It was dedicated to Pelops. The wall that enclosed the shrine was pentagonal. It was built on a levee, two meters high, 40 meters long and 30 meters wide. In the middle of the grove there was a statue and an altar. It should be noted here that the sacrifices were performed not over the altar but over a pit, because Pelops was worshipped as a man, not as a god.

Pelops was the most respected hero of the Eleans, just as Zeus was the most worshipped god.

4.1. Pelopeion — Hippodameion — House of Oinomaos

Oinomaos, Hippodameia and Pelops are three names that are connected with the early history of Olympia and the Olympic Games. Evidence of this is offered by many facts. For example, on the first pediment of the temple of Zeus there is a representation of the earliest tradition associated with these three persons. Also, the whole area, Peloponese, was named for Pelops.

Further, within the Altis, special sacred areas were established for Pelops and Hippodameia. In addition, the grave of Oinomaos was preserved beside the Kladeos river, opposite the Gymnasium. Also, Hippodameion was considered to be a sacred area in which the remains of Hippodameia were buried and each year local women used to offer sacrifices there.

The exact position of the Hippodameion has been

subject to controversy among archaeologists. Most probably, it was located on the eastern side of the Altis, to the west of the Stoa of Echo. On the other hand, the position of the Pelopeion has been established with accuracy. It lay between the Heraion and the great temple.

5. The Philippeion

This structure lies at the back of the Heraion and was built by Philippos the second, king of Macedonia, shortly after the battle of Chaironeia (338 B.C.).

However, two years after the beginning of the construction, Philippos died, and the building was completed by his son, Alexander the Great.

The Philippeion is a circular, peripteral structure, encircled by eighteen columns of Ionic style. It consists of the main temple and a stoa.

The interior of the temple was decorated with twelve

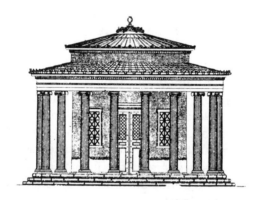

The Philippeion, a reconstruction.

The Philippeion as it is today.

Corinthian half-columns. There were five gold and ivory statues placed by Alexander the Great. The statues depicted Alexander the Great, his parents, Philippos and Olympiàs, and his forefathers. These statues were created by the Athenian sculptor Leochares.

6. The Prytaneion of the Eleans

THe Prytaneion was located to the north-west of the Altis. It was a square building. Each side was 32.80 meters

In the Prytaneion dined the official guests and the Olympic victors.

long. The building was divided into two parts. In the southern part there was the sacred hearth with its continually burning fire. This ever burning fire traces the origin of the Olympic flame that we know today. The northern part constituted the official dining place of the Eleans. It was here that all banquets were given.

7. The Metroon

This temple, which lies near the treasuries of the cities, was devoted to Kybele of Rea mother of the Gods. It was built during the 4th century B.C. It is 20.67 meters long,

The Metroon, a reconstruction.

10.62 meters wide, and 7.50 meters tall. It is a peripteral temple, enclosed by eleven and six Doric columns along its long and short sides, respectively. Like the other temples, it was divided into three parts, the **pronaos,** the main temple, and the **opisthodomos.**

Within the Metroon there was no statue of Kybele, since the temple was used for the cults of the Roman emperors. Therefore, many statues of them were set up inside the Metroon. For example, there were the statues of Claudius, Titus, Cesar, and others.

On the east side of the Metroon, the bases of the **Zanes,** the bronze statues of Zeus, have been preserved along the terrace of the treasuries, between the Metroon and the stadium.

The Metroon today.

.It is likely that this temple was demolished by the Byzantines, since some partly restored remains of it were found on the east side of the Byzantine wall.

7.1. Zanes

Zanes were called the copper statues of Zeus that were made by using the revenue from the fines imposed on athletes who violated the rules of the Olympic Games. The statues were placed, past the **Metroon,** before the entrance to the stadium, so that the athletes could see them and keep fresh in their minds the implications of infringing the rules. Six of the Zanes were built during the 90th Olympiad (384 B.C.) with the fines paid by the boxer Eupolos of Thessaly, and the boxers he had brided, Agetor of Arcadia and Prytanis of Kyzikos. It is also said that Sarapion of Alexandria was fined in A.D. 25 for quitting the Games the day before the event in which he was supposed to complete, because he felt he could not take the stress of competition.

The Zanes were sixteen and this serves as evidence of the fact that during the long history of the Olympic Games the rules were seldom broken. Unfortunately, only their bases have been preserved.

8. The Stoa of Echo or Poikile Stoa

This was a long stoa that constituted the eastern boundary of the sanctuary. It was 97.81 meters long and 9.81 meters wide. It had a base and steps of marble and was beautifully decorated. The spectators had an excellent view of the various ceremonies that used to take place in the sanctuary. The above stoa got its name from its magnificient acoustics. More specifically, the Stoa of Echo was also called Heptaëchos, because sounds re-echoed seven times in it.

It was built by Philippos of Macedonia, during the second half of the 4th century B.C.

9. The Nike (victory) of Paionios

Among the various statues and sculptures that were placed in the eastern side of the temple of Zeus, the best was the statue of **Nike** (the Greek word for victory), a work of the great sculptor Paionios of Thrace.

It is interesting ot note here that the concept of **Nike** (victory) was not an intangible quantity for the Greeks; on the contrary, the Greeks conceived victory as a concrete, tangible concept. This view of victory is amply evidenced by the large number of sculptures portraying Nike as a goddess. The **Nike** by Paionios was dedicated by the Messenians and the Naupaktians who beat the Spartans in the battle of Sphacteria, in 425 B.C. In this sculptural masterpiece, Paionios shows the goddess **Nike,** with her wings open and her dress spread out, descending from heaven to earth.

The Nike (Victory) of Paionios.

A copy of the Nike of Paionios, placed next to the original statue and, meausuring one fifth of the original's size.

The Nike of Paionios with its base.

B. Outside of the Altis were:

1. The south stoa

This stoa lies to the south of the Bouleuterion and was built during the 4th century B.C. It was 80.60 meters long and 14 meters wide. It formed the southern boundary of the sanctuary. According to one view, the south stoa was used as a marketplace.

2. The Bouleuterion

The Bouleuterion, lying to the south of the temple of Zeus, consists of three adjoining buildings. It is the place in which the Olympic House assembled, the money was

The Bouleuterion.

kept, and the various administrative documents were preserved. Also it was the place in which the conventions of the Hellanodikai took place. Finally, in one of the three buildings, there was the altar of Zeus Horkios, on which the athletes swore the statutory oath shortly before the beginning of the Games.

3. The Leonidaion

The Leonidaion was an immense, magnificient, rectangular building, 80.18 meters long and 73.51 meters wide.

The building was surrounded by an Ionic collonade on the outside, consisting of 138 columns, each of which was 5.56 meters tall.

The Leonidaion was named for its architect, Leonidas

The Leonidaion was the official guest-house during the Olympic Games.

of Naxos. It had comfortable rooms with beautifully decorated walls, and served as a guest house. Originally, it was intended to accomodate the official guests and distinguished visitors like kings, ambassadors and tyrants. However, during the Roman domination of the area, the building was used as a residence for Roman officials.

4. The Theokoleon

The Theokoleon is a rectangural building that lies south of the **palaistra.** This building served as the official house of the **Theokoloi,** the priests of Olympia who were in charge of the sanctuary. The selection of the **Theokoloi** was done every four years, that is their term lasted for exactly one Olympiad.

5. The Heroon

This building lies to the west of the Theokoleon. It resembles a circle inscribed in a square. The diameter of the circle is eight meters. According to one opinion, the Heroon housed the seers of Olympia.

The Heroon is thought to have been dedicated to the honor of some anonymous hero.

An inscription reading "heroos", preserved in the Museum of Olympia.

The Palaistra.

The Gymnasium. The training area of the athletes. Even pentathlon exercises could be performed here. On the right we see the exedra of the Herodes Atticus.

6. The Palaistra

The Palaistra was a large square building, 60 meters on each side, with many rooms. It was built in the 3rd century B.C. The building encompassed a yard in which the training of the wrestlers, pankratiasts and boxers used to take place. The yard was encircled by Doric columns which formed an archade with the interior walls of the building and thus provided an indoor training area for the athletes during rainy weather. There were also some rooms in which the athletes could take care of their bodies. Thus there was the **elaiothesion** (oiling-room), the **konisteirion** (dusting-room), a swimming pool, etc. Finally, there were classrooms in which the young athletes were taught the techniques of the various athletic events.

7. The Gymnasion

The Gymnasion was an ample, orthogonal, outdoor field that included three archades of which the eastern one was 210.51 meters long and 11.78 meters wide, and served as a track for running and pentathlon practice.

8. The Roman Thermai

The Roman Thermai were heated bathrooms, built during the time of Nero. They also served as rooms for changing. The mosaic floors of the Thermai are of considerable historic and artistic interest.

9. The Exedra of Herodes Atticus

Herodes Atticus was a well known philosopher and orator, and a teacher of Markus Avrelius. He was extremely rich and turned out to be the greatest benefactor of Olymia. From A.D. 141 to A.D. 157, he erected the Aqueduct of Olympia. The waters of springs that were located up to ten kilometers from the sanctuary were channeled into the Exedra. This was semicircular in shape and was placed above the cistern of the Aqueduct. The face of the Exedra was decorated by Herodes with statues of members of the imperial family. More specifically there were statues depicting Antonius Pius, Aimelius Avrelius, Antonius' wife Faustina, as well as Marcus Avrelius' wife. Later, the Eleans placed another fifteen statues depicting members of the family of Herodes Atticus.

10. The Stadium

The stadium of Olympia, the biggest in ancient Greece, was the place in which all of the Olympic events, except the horse and chariot races, took place. It was built in the 4th century B.C. It was rectangular in shape, 212 meters long and 30.70 meters wide. The running track was 192.27 meters, that is equal to the distance covered by the athletes in the stadion race. On the one side, the stadium was enclosed by the hill of Kronion. Thus, artificial slopes were built opposite the hill in order to enclose the other three sides. In this way, the stadium could hold as many as 45.000 spectators.

Initially, there were no seats on the embankments of

The stadium of Olympia. This was the competition area during the Games. The track is 192.27 meters long between the starting and finishing lines, that is equal to one Olympic "stadion". Opposite the exedra of the Hellanodikai is still preserved the altar of the godess Demeter Chamine. From this point, the priestess of the godess watched the Games.

the stadium and, as a result, the spectators used to sit on the ground. Of course, there were seats for some priviledged people. For example, the judges sat on the specially built **exedra of the Hellanodikai.** Also, there was a special seat for the priestess of Demeter Chamyne on the north side of the stadium.

11. The Krypte

The **Krypte** was a narrow, vaulted corridor, 32.10 meters long, 3.70 meters wide and 4.45 meters tall, that constituted the official entrance through which the athletes entered the stadium. It lies to the north of the Stoa of Echo.

The krypte. A covered corridor that connects the Altis with the stadium.

12. The Hippodrome

The hippodrome, in which the horse and chariot races were held, had a length of four studes (769.08 motors) and a width of 320 meters. The length of its perimeter was eight stades.
The hipodrome has not been excavated. It is most likely that a large part of it has been washed away by the floodings of the Alephios river.

13. The Treasuries

The treasuries were small Doric temples, consisting of a square room and a small **prodomos** resembling a **pronaos**. They were dedicated by the Greek cities, primarily the Colonies and Sicily, during the 6th and 5th centuries B.C. The main function of the treasuries was to house valuable dedications.

Treasury of Gela

It was built in 562 B.C. by the inhabitants of Gela, a city in Sicily. The architects were probably Sicilian. This treasury had two pediments, one of which was visible from the area of the stadium and the other form the Altis.

Treasury of Megara

It was constructed in the 6th century B.C. and resembled a Doric temple. On the pediment of this treasury there

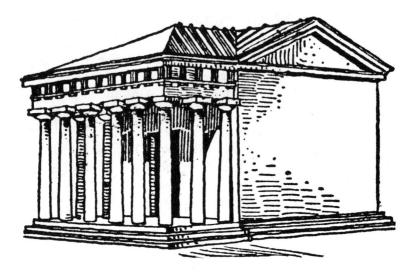

Treasury of Gela

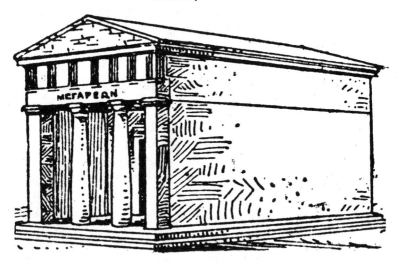

Treasury of Megara

was a bas-relief representing the fight between gods and giants, as well as the struggle between Herakles and Acheloos.

Treasury of Metopontion

It was built by the people of Metapontion, a city in southern Italy. It contained luxurious dedications which are refered to by Pausanias.

Inside the treasury there was a statue of Endymion. Also there were 32 gold-plated containers and various instruments for the performance of sacrifices.

Treasury of Selinous

This was one of the oldest treasuries, its construction dating back to between 550-500 B.C. It was dedicated by the residents of Selinous. Inside the treasury there was a statue of Dionysos. The head and limbs of the statue were made of ivory.

Treasury of Kyrene

It was the smallest treasury, built by the people of Kyrene, a fact evidenced by an inscription that was found during the excavations.

Treasury of Sybaris

Only a small part of this treasury is still preserved. It

was constructed in 510 B.C., after the destruction of the city of Sybaris by the city of Croton.

Treasury of Byzantion

Parts of the representations that existed on the pediment of this treasury are now preserved in the Museum of Olympia.

Treasury of Epidamnos

In the front part of this treasury there were four columns. Part of a bas-relief representing a rider is now preserved in the Museum.

Treasury of Syracuse

This treasury was the work of three architects, Pythaeos, Antiphilos, and Megakleus, according to the historian Pausanias. It included various dedications of Gelon.

Finally there are two more treasuries the origins of which have not been identified.

Third and second treasuries

These two treasuries are not mentioned by Pausanias because at that time they had virtually been covered by the exedra of Herodes Atticus. The third treasury had two columns while the second had three columns.

Treasury of Sikyon

It was built during the beginning of the 5th century B.C., in the Doric style. Its foundations and upper part were made of hight-quality stone. The pronaos had two columns and the roof was covered by marble tiles.

Almost all its constituent parts are preserved today so that it can be easily reconstructed. Inside this treasury were precions votive offerings, three trays, a knife belonging to Pelops and various other objects.

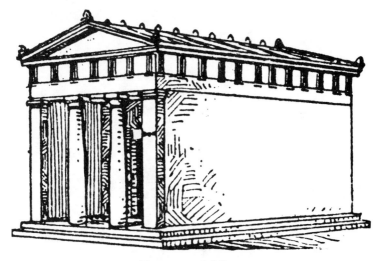

Treasury of Sikyon

Reconstruction: the Heraion, the exedra, and the Treasuries.

6. THE MODERN OLYMPIA

6.1. Ruins — Excavations

In the antiquity, Olympia was an immense building complex that included a·chain of architectual, sculptural, and decorative masterpieces. Imposing temples, magnificient graves of mythical kings, numerous altars, more than three thousand statues, a great stadium, luxurious hotels, marvelous edifices, artistic representations, bas-reliefs, and mosaic works constituted the glory and glare of Olympia. It is interesting to note here that Pausanias devoted two whole books to describe the works of art that saw in Olympia.

Today, after the Gothic raids of the 4th century, the edicts of Theodosius II, in A.D., 426 ordering the destruction of the temples, the force of the earthquakes of A.D. 522 and 551, and the floodings of Kladeos, only a few vestiges brought to surface by the excavations of meticulous archaeologists have been discovered and preserved.

Thanks to efforts spanning a period of more than two centuries, the German historian Ernest Kurt instructed and

A partial view of the excavations.

William Derpfeld
German architect, one of the first who
showed interest in excavating Olympia.

supervised about three thousand workers for six years, from September 22, 1875 to March 8, 1891, and excavated the area of ancient Olympia to a depth of seven meters, thus discovering thirty statues, thirteen thousand copper articles, six thousand coins of which 1.300 gold ones, four hundred inscriptions, one thousand clay objects, 130 sculptures, and forty monuments.

Ernest Kurt.
Famous German archaeologist and historian. A great researcher of ancient Greek ruins was in charge of the major excavations at Olympia.

7. THE MODERN OLYMPIC GAMES

7.1. Revival of the Games

For 1169 years, from 776 B.C. to A.D. 393 the Olympic Games were held in their birthplace. Then, following an edict by the byzantine Emperor Theodosius, the Games were abolished for fifteen hundred years. After the excavations at Olympic and the revival of the Olympic spirit, a Frenchman, Baron de Coubertin, who had worked for years to establish the modern Olympics, managed to get together in an athletic conference in 1894 the representatives of 13 countries and obtain a unanimous decision for the revival of the Games in Athens, Greece, in 1896. The countries that took part in the conference were Greece, France, England, Italy, U.S.A., Sweden, Belgium, Hungary, Australia, Holland, Spain, and Bohemia. Coubertin achieved with his efforts a place not only in the Olympic family but also in human history, since the Olympic idea represents the purity of athletic and artistic competition and illuminates the brotherhood of man.

Pierre de Coubertin
To this great French idealist and humanist belongs the credit for
the revival of the Olympic Games, as an institution that promotes
peace and understanding among the peoples of the world. Pierre
de Coubertin made it again possible for humans to gain the Olym-
pic victory. Thus, now, in his seventies, he is crowned with a
branch of laurel.

7.1a. Commemorative Column

At a distance of fifty meters from the entrance to the area of the excavations, we meet in a fenced area a column erected by the Olympic Committee in order to Commemorate the personality of Baron de Coubertin, the man who revived the modern Olympic Games.

In this column is preserved the heart of Pierre de Coubertin, according to his wish.

7.2. Organization and holding of the Games

The Olympic Games are held every four years and constitute the most important athletic event in the world. Officially, only amateur that is non-professional athletes are allowed to participate and compete in the events of the summer and winter Olympics. It should be noted at this point that contrary to the ancient Greek Olympic Games whose character was religious, the modern Games are a purely athletic event, aiming at the promotion of peace and friendy competition among the participating athletes and nations.

Each Olympiad begins with the parade of the athletes in the Olympic stadium in which arrives the athlete that carries the Olympic flame. The Olympic flame is kept lit during the Games and symbolizes the ever-burning torch of the ancient athletic ideal. The carrying of the Olympic flame from ancient Olympia to the Olympic Stadium of the country in which the Games will be held, has the form of a relay event. At the inauguration ceremony of each Olympiad, the head of state of the host country declares the Games open and there follows the raising of the Olympic flag, a white flag depicting five circles, colored blue, yellow, black, green and red. This flag was officially introduced in the 1920 Olympics held in Antwerp.

The end of the Games is declared by a judge who at the same time invites the athletes to participate in the next Olympic Games.

The Olympic oath is recited by an athlete of the host country. The oath was written by Baron de Coubertin.

A. The summer Olympiad

The summer Olympiad contains twenty two events that are classified into the following categories.

a) Track and field events, b) combat and shooting events, c) gymnastics and weight lifting, d) water sports, e) modern pentathlon, f) equestrian events.

In order for a sport to be included in the Olympic program, it must be performed in a minimum of twenty five countries. This is why some otherwise popular events like base-ball and gulf have not yet been included in the Olympics.

1. Track and Field events

These contain run, jump, throw, and walk events, group events like handball, football, hockey, and volleyball, and cycling.

2. Combat events and shooting

In this category we have fencing, wrestling (freestyle and Greco-Roman), boxing, judo and shooting.

3. Gymnastics and weight lifting

In these we include gymnastics (combined exercises, floor exercises, horizor*al bars, rings etc.) and weight lifting.

4. Swimming, diving, rowing, sailing and water-polo

5. Modern Pentathlon

6. Equestrian events

These include team and individual show jumping and dressage and treee day events.

B. The Winter Olympiad

The Winter Olympiad was established in 1924. It is held every four years, like the summer Olympiad, at a different place from that of the summer Olympiad. Foi example, the winter Olympics of 1964 were held in Insbruk, Austria, while the summer ones took place in Tokyo. Likewise the winter Olympics of 1968 were held in Grenoble while the summer ones in Mexico City.

It should be noted that the summer Olympics, as they are not restricted to the holding of only a few winter sports but include a large number of athletic events, enjoy greater prestige than do the winter Olympics.

7.3. Regulations of the Olympic Games

Participation in the Games is subject to strict rules. The participants are required to be amateur athletes and their participation must first be approved by the Olympic

Committee of their respective countries. More specifically, in order to be allowed to take part in the Games, the athletes must:

a) Not have ever received a cach prize of more than $50 for their athletic performance.

b) Not have ever used their athletic capacity in order to achieve monetary or other advantages.

c) Not have ever expressed the wish to turn to professional athletics.

d) Not have ever been hired as paid instructors of their sport.

e) Not have received a scholarship on the basis of their athletic ability.

The athletes that participate in the Games must be citizens of the country that they represent. Each country is allowed to send up to three of its athletes to participate in each Olympic competition. However, we should state at this juncture that the Olympic rules and regulations are often revised and adapted to the changing circumstances.

Gold, silver, and copper medals go to the athletes that have, respectively, finished first, second, and third, in a competition.

The supreme administrative organ of the Olympic Games is the International Olympic Committee (IOC). Its headquarters is in Lausane, Switzerland. The IOC is responsible for the normal conduct of the Games, the maintemance of the Olympic ideal and spirit, and the possible amendment of the rules governing the Games. Also, the IOC selects the place in which each Olympiad will be held. As soon as the place is chosen, the responsibility for the holding of the Olympic Games lies solely with the National Olympic Committee of the host country.

7.4. The Olympic Flag

The five partially overlapping circles of the Olympic flag are supposed to represent the friendly ties among the five continents, America, Europe, Asia, Africa and Australia. Another version has it that the five circles represent the five precursors of the Olympic Games in ancient times, the Courete brothers, who used to hold athletic competitions.

7:5. The Olympic Flame

The custom of carrying the Olympic flame from Olympia to the Olympic stadium of the host country was first started in 1936, when the Germans carried the flame from Olympia to Berlin. This symbolic gesture has been repeated ever since.

The flame is lighted in Olympia, in the altar of Hera which is located in front of the Temple of Hera. The kindling temperature is secured with the help of a metalic concave lens that properly focuses the sunrays. Subsequently the first torch is lighted and carried by a runner through the stadium of Olympia to a marble altar in front of the monument of Baron de Coubertin. From this point the flame is carried all the way to Athens by means of runners who are replaced every one kilometer. From Athens the flame travels to the host country by any appropriate means of transportation.

The priestess lights the first torch.

The first priestess holds the amphora with the Olympic flame that was given her by the priestess of Hestia, and proceeds along with the other priestesses in the stadium.

Priestesses in procession for the delivery of the Olympic flame.

A beautiful archaic ceremony takes place in Olympia for the delivery of the Olympic flame.

Ceremony in the stadium for the kindling of the Olympic torch.

The priestess of Hestia carries the Olympic flame in order to hand it to the first torch runner.

The priestess of Hestia delivers the Olympic flame to the first runner who in turn, will light the Olympic altar.

The altar of the Olympic flame.

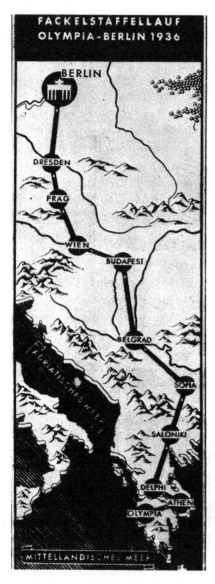

The route that followed the Olympic flame in 1936 (Berlin Olympiad). It was the first time that the flame was carried from Olympia to the Olympic stadium of the host country.

The Olympic torch relay, London 1948.

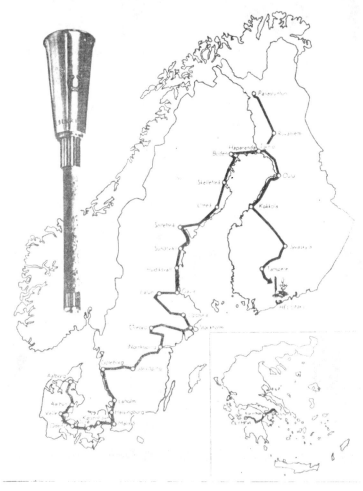

The Olympic torch relay, Helsinki 1952.

The Olympic flame, Melbourne 1956.

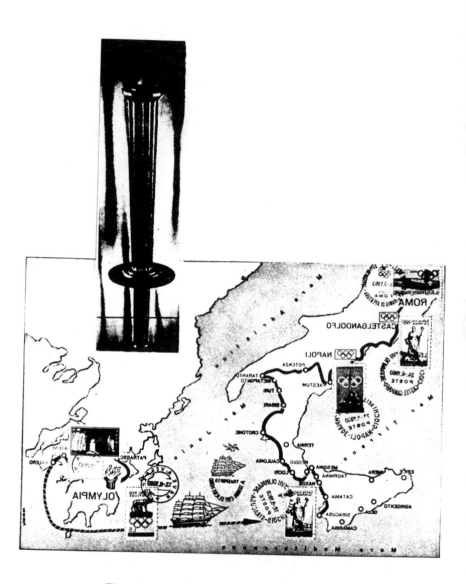

The Olympic flame torch relay, Rome 1960.

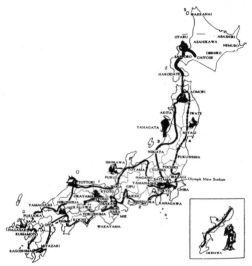

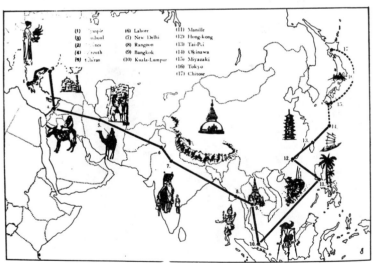

The Olympic torch relay, Tokyo 1964.

The Olympic torch relay, Mexico 1968.

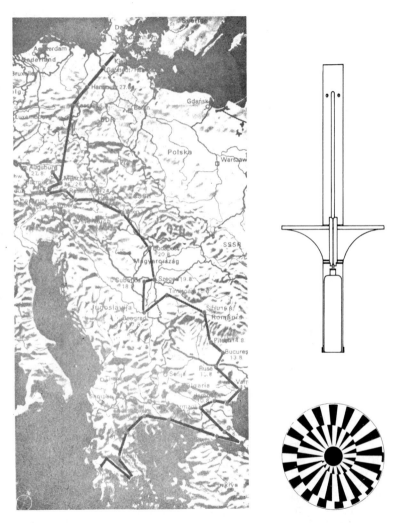

The Olympic torch relay, Munich 1972.

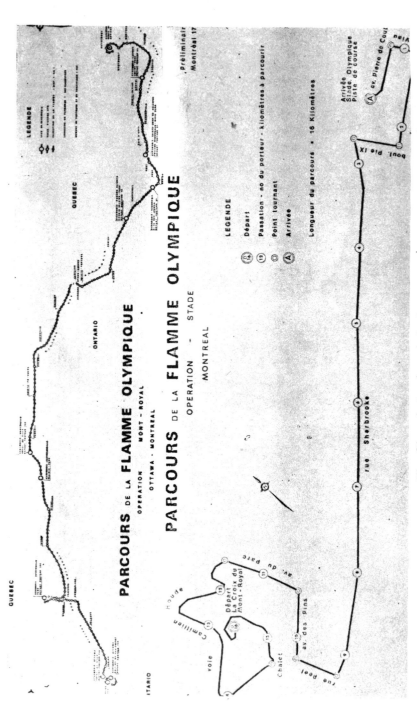

The Olympic torch realy in Canada 1976.

On the occasion of the ceremony for the arrival of the Olympic flame in the stadium of Athens (1976), Constantine Tsatsos, then President of the Greek Repuplic said: "This flame brings a message from as far back as 26 centuries. The message of noble competition, peace and humanism. Let this flame enlighten all the people of the world".

7.6. OLYMPIC HYMN

Immortal ancient spirit, whole
some father of the beautiful,
the great and the true,
come down and shine right here,
in the glory of your land and heaven.

KOSTIS PALAMAS
(Famous Greek Poet)

7.7. Extracts from the history of the Olympic Games

1. Olympia

The valley of Olympia was chosen by the ancient Greeks as the place for the holding of classical Greece's most renowned athletic celebration, the Olympic Games, a festivity dedicated to Zeus.

The landscape of Olympia was the most attractive of all Greece, because of its vegetation and pleasant serenity.

155

2. Character of the Games

The ancient Greeks were known to be worshippers of beauty and virtue. In this context, the Games should be viewed as a festivity aiming at elevating the human beings to the sphere of the good, the gentle and the beautiful. The Games began as a local, religious and athletic institution that conquered the whole world and reached its present state of global recognition.

3. Olympia — Panhellenic athletic center

Olympia was the greatest national shrine of ancient Greece, equalled only by the shrine of Delphi. The subsequent holding of the Olympic Games at that side, helped make Olympia a symbol of togetherness and brotherhood.

4. Monuments of ancient Olympia

Ancient Olympia is one of the best known cities of the antiquity.

The area of the sanctuary was full of masterpieces, like temples, altars, dedications, statues and structures for the holding of athletic events. The excavations have brought to surface much of the artistic wealth of ancient Olympia.

5. Olympia as a Museum of Greece

Thanks to the efforts of Greek and foreign archaeologists, Olympia possesses today one of the richest museums in Greece.

6. Mount Kronion

From the slopes of Kronion one has excellent view of the sanctuary, the ruins of the temples and other monuments. With the help of her or his imagination, the sightseer may reconstruct in her or his mind the organization and atmoshpere of the Games.

7. Origin of the Games

The various versions of the origin of the Games fluctuates between myth and reality, and is lost in the times preceding recorded history. It is certain, however, that the Games rose from the natural inclination of the ancient Greeks to compete and the gradual shaping of the view that bodily exercise improves both physical and mental health.

8. Participation in the Games

So great was the prestige of the Games that the athletes participated in great numbers and the crowds packed the stadium of Olympia to watch the competitions. Thales and Cheilon, two of Greece's famous "wise men" went to Olympia to watch the Games and died there, during the festivities. In particular, Thales died of exhaustion caused by the hardships of his long trip from Miletos to Olympia, while Chilon died of a heart attack caused by intense emotion, as his son was being crowned Olympic victor.

9. Women

Women were not allowed to participate in the Olympic Games or to watch them as spectators. However they could be declared Olympic victors in the equestrian events, since it was the owner of the winning chariot or horses, not the rider, that was pronounced victor.

10. Olympiads

The Olympic Games were considered to embody the concept of the brotherhood of man. Olympia was in this sense a workshop in which world peace was promoted.

11. Olympic Events

During the first thirteen Olympiads the main Olympic event was that of running, and more specifically the **stadion** race, corresponding to the modern race of 100 meters. In 724 B.C. the **diaulos** race was introduced, roughly corresponding to the modern 200 m. race, and in 720 B.C., the **dolichos** race (2,000 m) was introduced. Then, in 708 B.C. appeared the wrestling and pentathlon events, in 688 B.C. boxing was introduced, in 680 we have the tethrippon (four-horse) race, and in 648 B.C. the pankration became an additional event.

The boys' running and wrestling events were introduced in 632 B.C. Finally, in 396 B.C. the hearlds' and trumpeters' competitions were first held.

The runners always ran barefoot. In the earliest times they wore a kind of loin cloth, but later they ran naked.

The first day of the Games was dedidated to various ceremonies, rituals and sacrifices. It was during this day that the athletes and the **Hellanodikai** (umpires) swore the official oath at the Bouleuterion (Council-House) in front of the statue of Zeus Horkios. It should be noted here that there had been very few cases of athletes or Hellanodikai who actually broke their oath and violated the Olympic rules.

The second day was devated to the boys' events. Boys' running and wrestling was introduced in 632 B.C. and boys' pugilism in 616 B.C. Pindar refers with admiration to three boys, the wrestler Alkimedon of Aigina, the boxer Agesidamos and the runner Asopihos of Orhomenos.

Some of the most eminent runners in Olympic history were Argeus of Argos, Dandis of Argos and Ladas of Sparta.

The race in Armor was first introduced in 520 B.C. and was held during the fourth day of the Olympiad.

Wrestling was greatly admired by the Greeks because of its sophisticated techniqes and practical importance.

Among the regulations of the games was one that seems alien to the modern concepts of athletic competitions, the rule of the **ephedreia** ("the bye"). In particular, in events in which the athletes were drawn to compete in pairs, line the boxing, wrestling and pankration, it often happened that the number of participating athletes was odd. As a result one competitor would be left over with an oppanent. He was not excluded but was considered fortunate enough to compete only in the final. This man was called ephedros meaning "the man waiting".

The most spectacular and prestigious competitions were the equestrian events. The race course became in essence an area for demonstrating one's material and political power. The chariot races were: the **tethrippon** (four -horse, chariot), the **apene** (a chariot pulled by two mules), the **synoris** (a chariot pulled by a pair of horses), the **tethrippon for foals,** and the **synoris for foals.**

Because winner of a race was declared the owner of the horses and not the respective rider, the equestrian events made it possible for women to be declared Olympic victors.

12. The Olympic victory

This was the greatest possible glory that a human could reach in the ancient Greek world. No other feat or achievement could equal the glory that accompanied an Olympic victory.

13. Olympia as a symbol of Unity and Peace

During the Games all differences that separated the Greek cities-states were forgotten. As a result Olympia became a very potent vechicle of understanding, negotiation and peace among the Greek. The spirit of Olympia was this: a belief in human nature, in bodily strength, in moral worth, in democracy, in peace and love. Likewise, in the modern Olympiads, the flags of all countries in the world appear together, along with the white Olympic flag with the five overlapping circles, representing the friendship of the five continents of the globe.

8. THE MUSEUM OF OLYMPIA

The Museum of Olympia is located on the west side of the Kladeos river, on the hill of Eratinos. It was constructed in 1886 with the financial help that was made available by the Greek benefactor Andreas Syngros. In this museum one will find virtually all the archaeological findings that resulted from the excavations of the German archaeologists. Among these findings were statues, statuettes, athletic and military instruments, quills, altars, inscriptions, samples of all kinds of columns, helmets, tripods, shields, etc.

The Museum consists of the prodomos, the central hall, the hall of Hermes, and two side wings.

As one enters the Museum through main entrance, one meets on one's left the bust of Hernest Kurt, the archaeologist in charge of the excavations that brought to surface the findings that are exposed in the museum. On the right side of the prodomos across the main entrance are the statues of Various Roman emperors. In the central hall are placed the statues that used to decorate the pediments of the prestigious temple of Zeus, as well as the statue of Nike (victory) of Paionios.

The Museum

The middle of the west pediment.

On the walls of the main corridor we see representations of the twelve feats of Hercules. Originally, these representations decorated the temple of Zeus. More specifically, the east pediment illustrates the mythical chariot race between Oinomaos and Pelops. The west pediment represents a Centauromachy.

According to a myth, Perithoos, a king of the Lapiths, invited the Centaurs to his wedding to Deidameia. Also invited to the wedding was the well-known ancient Greek hero Theseus.

During the wedding ceremony the Centaurs attempted to abduct Deidameia. The Lapiths, with the help of Theseus, got engaged in a fierce fight and managed to kill the Centaurs. In the middle of the pediment stands Apollo, who was the father of both the Lapiths and the Centaurs. His head, is turned to the left and his right arm extended.

The remains of the metops that represented the achievements of Hercules we see on the left of the large entrance, the following:

1) The Stymphalian Birds, wild birds with copper beaks, that lived in the Stymphalian lake.

2) The Hydra, a giant snake with nine heads, of which the middle one was immortal. Hercules managed, with the help of his friend Iolaos to kill the snake.

3. The Lion of Nemea.

4. Hippolyte's Belt.

5. The Deer of Keryne.

6. The cleansing of the Augean stable.

7. The capturing of the Cerberus.

8. The abduction of Diomedes' horses.

9. The capturing of the boar of Erymantus.

The Hermes of Praxiteles, the famous statue that was found in the temple of Hera, shows Hermes holding in his left arm a child, the infant Dionysos.

Apollo (from the representations of the west pediment).

Statue of a woman (from the representations of the east pediment).

165

Deidameia (West Pediment).

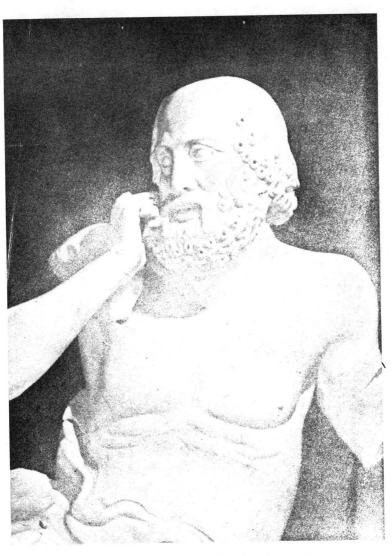

The thinking old man (East Pediment).

Hermes of Praxiteles.

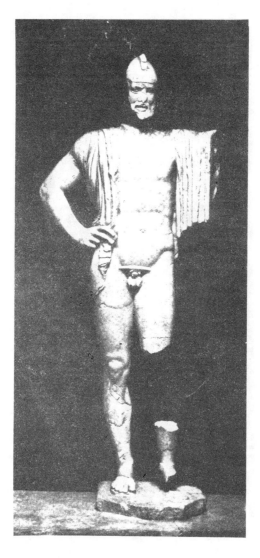

Oinomaos (East Pediment).

Pelops (East Pediment).

East Pediment.

East Pediment.

Hippodameia (East Pediment).

Sterope (East Pediment).

The beautiful Lapith woman

Head of the beautiful Lapith woman.

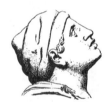

West Pediment, angular aspect.

Head of Kladeos.

The preserved foot of Hermes.

The stymphalian birds.

The capture of the wild dog.

The Lion of Nemea.

The Golden Apples of the Hesperides. On the right we see Atlas holding the apples. Herakles, in the middle, carriers the tremendous burden of the sky. Athena stands behind him, helping him.

The cleansing of the stables of Augeus.

The bull of Knossos.

A series of Roman statues in the exedra.

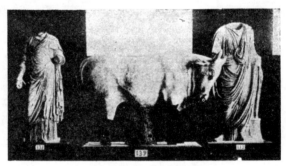

Regilla? Bull. Rode bearer.

Titus.

Tiberius Claudius

Poppaia Savine

Head of the statue of Poppaia Savine

Hadrian, Roman Emperor.

Agrippina, mother of Nero.

A clay complex of Zeus and Ganymedes. It was placed on the pediment of an unknown small building in the Altis. It was a work of rare delicacy, 470 B.C. (approximately).

The stone of Bybon

This stone weighs almost 150 kilos and has an inscription on it that reads:

"Bybon, a son of Pholas lifted me with one hand above his head".

The stone is now in the Museum of Olympia.

The inscribed stone of Bybon

9. A SHORT HISTORY OF OLYMPIC GAMES PAST

1. ATHENS, 1896

The first Modern Olympic Games were held in Athens, Greece, on March 25, 1896. The Games took place in the marble-stadium of Athens, the restoration of which was due to the Greek benefactor George Averof.

The organization of this Olympiad was satisfactory. Twelve nations were represented, including Greece, France, England, Switzerland, Germany, Hungary and the United States.

Princeton's Robert S. Garrett won two gold and two silver medals, including the gold for the discus throw, an achivement that startled the Greek spectators. Bob Garret had never seen a real discus and had been practicing with an iron fascimile. His winning throw was 29.15 meters.

The contest that really mattered to the Greeks was the marathon that was finally won by a young Greek water hauler, Spyros Loues. The crowd went into a frenzy when Prince George II jumped from the royal box and ran the last few meters by Loues' side.

The organizing committee of the Olympic Games of 1896.

The first meeting of the organizing committee of the 1896 Olympics that took place in Athens, Greece. Second from left, the Baron Pierre de Coubertin.

Athens 1896: The athletes are ready for the final of the 100-meter run. Second from the left is the American runner Burke who first used starting position shown in the picture. This impressed the spectators at the time. Gradually, Burke's method of starting a sprint race was adopted as the standard method.

Spyros Loues, the Greek winner of the Marathon in the 1896 Olympics. Loues will be the last torch bearer that will bring the Olympic flame in the Olympic stadium of Berlin, in 1936.

2. PARIS, 1900

In spite of a lot of sentiment to keep the Games in Athens permanently, Baron de Coubertin awarded the holding of the Second Olympiad to his home country, France. In fact, the Games became something of a side show to the Universal exhibition that was being held in Paris that year. Paris was not properly prepared to hold the Games not only because of lack of organization but also because the athletic spirit was not very developed among the French. There were achieved, however, some important

Paris 1900: The Olympic Games took place in the Hippodrome of Paris, in the forest of Boulogne. The 500-meter fence partially blocked the view. In general, the organization of the Games was poor.

world records. We should mention here the feat of a 19-year-old University of Pennsylvania student named Alvin C. Krazlein, who won four individual events, the 60 meter sprint, the 110 meter high hurdles, the 200 meter low hurdles and the running broad jump, setting world records in all four events.

Also, it should be pointed out that Krazlein's achievement was later eclipsed by his fellow American Ray C. Ewry, who won gold medals in all three standing jump events at Paris, the high jump, the broad jump and the hop, step and jump. Altogether, Ewry won ten Olympic victories in four Olympiads (1900, 1904, 1906, 1908).

Another American athlete, J. Flanagan won the hammer throw event with a throw of 167 ft. 4 in. Finally, M. Long of the U.S. team achieved 49.4 second in the 400-meter run.

In summary, some of the records achieved in Paris were later appreciated and rated as excellent, but the organization of this Olympiad was very disappointing.

The spectators were allowed to come into the field and interrupt the contests, there was no cinder track, the races were held on a park, and the discus and hammer throwers discovered that their best tries landed in a grove of trees.

3. ST. LOUIS, 1904

The American dominance of the previous two Olympiads made it natural to hold the third modern Olympiad in the U.S. However, as amateur athletes had to pay their own way to the event and St. Louis was just too far away and too hard to get to for most foreign athletes to bother with, only two European countries participated, Germany and

Hungary. This lack of international competition led again to the dominance of the American athletes. The superman Ewry won all the jump and vault events. Thomas Hicks won the marathon race. Another American, Fred Lorz, had arrived at the stadium fifteen minutes before Hicks and had already been acclaimed by the crowd when Hicks finished the race. However, it was revealed that Lorz had hitched a ride on a truck for part of the way.

4. ATHENS, 1906
INTERIM OLYMPIAD

The reluctance of other countries to assume the great cost of organizing an Olympiad and the view of Baron de Coubertin that the Olympic ideal needed a strong boost, led to the decision to hold an interim Olympics in Athens in 1906.

As in 1896, the huge stadium was filled every day and the event went off without any difficulties, surpassing all previous contests in the number of nations and athletes participating.

Present in the Games were the royal family of Greece, the king and Queen of England, the Prince and Princess of Wales and many other personalities of the time.

The event that drew most the attention of the audience was the Marathon race. The Greeks, however, failed to repeat the 1896 triumph of Spyros Loues as the competition was won by Shering, a Canadian athlete.

Below we present in tabular form a list of the Marathon winners from the first modern Olympiad to today.

1896 Athens, S. Loues, Greece, 2h. 58m. 50s

1900 Paris, M. Teato, France, 2h. 59m. 45s.
1904 St. Louis, T. Hicks, United States, 2h. 58m. 18s.
1906 Athens, Shering, Canada, 2h. 51m. 23s.
1908 London, J.J. Hayes, United States, 2h. 55m. 23.6s.
1912 Stockholm, K. McArthur, South Africa, 2h. 36m. 54.8s.
1920 Antwerp, H. Kolehmainen, Finland, 2h. 32m. 35.8s.
1924 Paris, A. Stenroos. Finland, 2h. 41m. 22.6s.
1928 Amsterdam, A. BEl Quafi, France, 2h. 32m. 57s.
1932 Los Angeles, J. Zabala, Argentina, 2h. 31m. 36s.
1936 Berlin, K. Son, Japan, 2h. 29m. 19.2s.
1948 London, D. Cabrera, Argentina, 2h. 34m. 51.6s.
1952 Helsinki, E. Zatopek, Czechoslovakia, 2h. 23m. 03.2s.
1956 Melbourn, A. Mimoun, France, 2h. 25m.
1960 Rome, A. Bikila, Ethiopia, 2h. 15m. 16.2s.
1964 Tokyo, A. Bikila, Ethiopia, 2h. 12m. 11.2s.
1968 Mexico City, M. Wolde, Ethiopia, 2h. 20m. 26.4s.
1972 Munich, F. Shorter, United States, 2h. 12m. 19.8s.
1976 Montreal, W. Cierpinski, E. Germany, 2h. 09m. 55s.
1980 Moscow, W. Cierpinski, E. Germany, 2h. 11m. 03s.

Below we present the translation of an extract from an April 1906 copy of the Greek daily "Esperini" in which the editor of the newspaper comments comments on the views expressed at the time by various European newspapers on the reasons why the Olympic Games should take peace permanently in Greece.

LAST MINUTE NEWS

THE OLYMPIC GAMES
ENTHUSIASTIC COMMENTS IN THE EUROPEAN PRESS
WHERE THE GAMES SHOULD TAKE PLACE
Berlin, April 13. The whole European Press publishes

enthusiastic articles about the Olympic Games that are currently taking place in Athens. In particular, a number of articles suggest that the Games must permently take place in Greece because they remind us of the fact that Greece has offered so much.

THE MEETING OF THE OLYMPIC COMMITTEES

ATHENS WILL BECOME THE PERMANENT HOST—CITY OF THE GAMES

It is certain that all foreing representatives, foremost among them the Swedish, Mr. Black, and the American, Mr. Sullivan, will propose Athens as the place in which the Olympic Games should take place in the future. The city of Athens possesses all facilities required for the sucessful organization of the Games.

5. LONDON, 1908

The organization of the London Olympics was very good. The English built a great stadium with a capacity of 100,000 spectators. Many new sports were introduced in the Olympic program, such sports as hockey, polo, and rowing. The British won this Olympiad, but it should be noted that in most races they did not have any foreign competitors since they concerned totally British sports.

The finish of the Marathon race was exciting. The Italian athlete Dorando, who led tha race, collapsed a few yards before the end and was helped by the British officials through the finish line. Later, however, the Italian was disqualified and the medal went to the American J. J. Hayes.

London 1908: The Italian Dorando collapsed a few meters before the finish line of the Marathon race. Subsequently, he was helped through the finish line but was later disqualified.

6. STOCKHOLM, 1912

The Swedes staged the best Olympic Games up until that time. Europe discovered with surpise that in Sweden lived the most athletic people in the world. Involvement with sport activities in Sweden was not the privilege of a small class of the population, but part of everyone's life.

The whole Olympiad was conducted fairly and with much finesse, so that no serious complains came from any of the twenty-six participating nations.

The Finnish athlete Kolehmainen won the 5,000, 8,000 and 10,000 meter runs.

It should be noted that the 5,000-meter run was first introduced at the Stockholm Olympiad. The South African McArthur, a great talent of that time, won the Marathon. A few yards before the end, McArthur fell down but managed to get up in time and pass first the finish line. The superathlete Jim Thorpe won two of the most difficult Olympic events, the five event pentathlon and the ten event decathlon. His performance in Stockholm has never been matched. However, a couple of years later, a Boston newspaper revealed that he had taken board money for playing

Stockholm 1912: The entry of the Swedish team. In the backround we see the Swedish royal family.

baseball one summer. The Amateur Athletic Union stripped Thorpe of his Olympic medals.

The Japanesse swimmer Kahanamoku won the 100-meter freestyle and actually introduced the swimming style that is known as "crawl".

7. ANTWERP, 1920

The First World War did not allow the holding of an Olympiad in 1916. The Games of 1920 in Antwerp, were held in an atmosphere of mistrust, nationalism and hatred. The Olympic ideal had suffered a serious setback, as the War had affected negatively the mentality of the people. In Antwerp, the Belgians tried to present something that would

Antwerp 1920: The commencement ceremony, with each country's team behind the respective flag.

help change this atmosphere, but there was no wide response on the part of the people.

In the Antwerp Olympic, the five-circle Olympic flag is introduced. The five circles symbolize the five continents. The idea of the flag belonged to Baron de Coubertin.

Britain sent a small team, while other European countries decided not to participate.

On the records front, we should mention here the Finnish Kolehmainen who won the Marathon, the other Finnish superman P. Nurbi, winner of the 10,000-meter run, and the American C. Paddock who earned the gold medal of the 100-meter run. Finland won the most medals and points, while the United States came second. However, the Americans dominated the swimming events.

8. PARIS, 1924

In 1924 the Games were again held in Paris, in a magnificient Olympic stadium. It is true to say that the 1924 Paris Olympics constituted a great leap forward in terms of athletic organization and athletic spirit. Also, this Olympiad showed vividly the importance of sports as a vehicle to bring different countries closer and hammer a new international understanding. In general, this was a monumental Olympiad.

In the 100, 400, and 800-meter runs the British Abrahams, Liddell, and Lowe, beat the American giants, much to everyone's surpise. Also, this was the Olympiad in which the star of the swimmer John Weissmuller of the United States shone brightly. Further, the Finnish Nurbi won the 1,500, and 5,000-meter runs achieving world

Paris 1924: Géo André swears the Olympic oath in front of the flags of the participating countries.

records of breathtaking dimensions. Another Finnish athlete, W. Ritola carried the 3,000-meter steeplechase and the 10,000 meter run. In soccer, Switzerland reached the final but lost to Uruguay.

9. AMSTERDAM, 1928

The Amsterdam 1928 Olympiad is remembered, among other things, as the Olympics in which track and field was added to the women's events.

Some great athletes marked with their performances this Olympiad. We should mention here the Canadian Wil-

Amsterdam 1928: The international Dutch soccer player Harry Denis swears the Olympic oath in front of the flags of the participating nations.

liaıns who won the 100 and 200-meter runs, the British Lowe and Burghley, winners, respectively of the 800-meter run and the 400-meter hurdles, and the American Houser, winner of the Discus throw.

The ideal of a brotherhood of man was revived in this Olympiad; the trauma of the First World War has been forgotten. The Olympic spirit is again winning the hearts and minds of the people.

10. LOS ANGELES, 1932

For the first time in the history of the Olympic Games, an Olympic village was constructed in Los Angeles, in

1932. This helped the athletes prepare themselves better, concentrate on their events, and rest quietly, away from the spectators. That was an Olympiad in which the United States dominated the majority of both men's and women's events. However, in swimming, the Japanese won five gold medals.

In particular, we should refer here to the Japanese swimmers Miyazaki (100-meter freestyle), Kitamura (1,500-meter freestyle), Kiyokawa (100-meter backstroke), and Tsuruta (200-meter backstroke), the United States sprinters Tolan (100 and 200-meter run) and Carr (400-meter run), and W. Miller who, after a dramatic competition beat the Japanese Nishida in the pole vault.

Los Angeles 1932: The Marathon race was exciting. Here we see the winner of the race Zabala of Argentina.

The Olympic village of Los Angeles was a model construction. It was the first time in Olympic history that the athletes lived far from the turmoil of the city.

The International Olympic Committee meets in Oslo (1935) and e-xamines various proposals for the coming Games.

11. BERLIN, 1936

This Olympiad was meticulously organized by Hitler's German Nazi government. During the Games, the Fuhrer attempted to prove his theory of Aryan superiority and saw his views shattered when Jesse Owens, an American black, won four gold medals.

It should be noted that it was during this Olympiad that the Olympic flame was for the first time carried from Olympia to Berlin, with the help of a long chain of torch-bearers. The torch was made from such materials as not to go out in the face of wind or rain. Spyros Loues, the 1896 Olympic victor of the Marathon was selected by the Germans to be the final torch-bearer who actually brought the flame within the Olympic stadium of Berlin.

Dr. Karl Ritter Von Half, president of the organising committee of the winter Olymplics (1936) welcomes in the Olympic Ski Stadium the athletes of the 28 participating countries.

12. LONDON, 1948

The Second World War suspended the Games for 12 years. However, shortly after the war, there was a rekindling of the Olympic spirit. In the London Games, the United States was represented with a very strong team and won most contests. This Olympiad would be remebered primarily because of two contestants. First, the great long-distance runner Emil Zatopek of Czechoslovakia, and Fanny Blankers-Koen, the "Flying Dutch-woman", who, at the age of thirty (and a mother of two children) picked up four gold medals (for the 100 and 200 meter races, the 90 meter hurdles and as a member of Holland's relay team).

13. HELSINKI, 1952

This Olympiad was excellently organized and is remembered among other things for the fact that Emil Zatopek, the superathlete from Czechoslovakia won the gold medals for the 5,000, the 10,000 and the Marathon races: Also, during this Olympiad, the Soviet Union made its first appearance.

14. MELBOURN, 1956

The United States dominated once more the Olympiad. B. Morrow won the 100 and 200 meter races, C. Jenkins the 400-meter run, T. Courtney the 800-meter race. The Soviet V. Kuts won the 5,000 and 10,000 meter races, while the Marathon gold went to the French A. Mimoun. A. Oerter of the United States won the Discus Throw, a victory that was to be repeated in the 1960 Rome Olympiad, and in the 1964 Tokyo Games. Australia dominated the swimming events, while the Soviet Union won the soccer gold.

15. ROME, 1960

This Olympiad would be remembered for three events. First, the Australian H. Elliott won the 1,500 meter race with an unprecedented 3m. 35.6s. Second, A. Bikila won the Marathon barefooted.

Third, the victory of W. Nieder of the United States in the Shot Put.

16. TOKYO, 1964

This was another very successful Olympiad. Again, the Americans dominated the Track and Field events. In particular, we should mention here B. Mills' victory in the 10,000 meter race, and B. Schul's victory in the 5,000 meter run. Also, the U. S. swimmer Don Schollander won four gold medals, a feat that was to be surpassed only by another American swimmer, M. Spitz in the 1972 Munich Olympics. Another athlete that would be rememberd was the Soviet V. Brumel who won the running High Jump.

17. MEXICO CITY, 1968

This Olympiad is mainly remembered for a record that

many experts have declared to be unbreakable for years to come: B. Beamon's (U. S.) breathtaking 29ft. 5-¾ (8 meters and 90 centimeters) in the Long Jump.

Also, we should mention the victories of the African athletes Keino (3,000 meter steeplechase), Gammoundi (5,000 meter run), Temon (10,000 meter run), and Wolde (Marathon).

18. MUNICH, 1972

This Olympiad was marked by its excellent organization and by the victories of M. Spitz (U. S.) in swimming, the Soviet V. Borzov in the 100 and 200 meter races, the African Keino (3,000 meter steeplechase), the Fin L. Viren in the 5,000 and 10,000 meter races, and the East Germany in the women's track and field events.

19. MONTREAL, 1976

This Olympiad was characterized by an Olympic village that was a marvel of architectural and technological perfection. Among the great athletes that participated in this Olympiad we will make reference here to the Cuban A. Juantorena who won the 400 and 800 meter races, the Romanian girl N. Comaneci who dominated the Gymnastics events, the Fin L. Viren who repeated his 1972 Olympic triumph, winning, the 5,000 and 10,000 meter races and the East German woman swimmer K. Ender who won five gold medals.

20. MOSCOW, 1980

Although well organized, the Moscow Olympiad was marred by the fact that, as a result of the Soviet invasion of Afghanistan, 56 countries decided not to participate in the Games.

Despite this, some interesting records were achieved. We mention here that the Ehtiopian M. Yifter won the 10,000 meter run, the 1976 Olympic victor of the Marathon W. Cierpinski of E. Germany repeated his feat, S. Ovett of Great Britain won the 800 meter race while his compatriot S. Coe won the 1,500 meter race, A. Wells of Great Britain

The kindling ceremony of the Olympic flame in ancient Olympia. We see the first priestess, Maria Moscholios.

won the 100 meter run, P. Mennea of Italy carried the 200 meter run, D. Thomson of Great Britain won the Decathlon, and the Soviet and East German women dominated women's track and field, with the exception of S. Simeoni of Italy who won the High Jump. Also the Soviets dominated cycling, volley ball, water polo, women's volley ball, and fencing.

The Olympic flame was lit not only in the Lenin Stadium but also in four other cities in which Olympic events will take place (Tallin, Kiev, Leningrad and Minsk). In the picture we see the ceremony at Minsk.

THE OLYMPIC GAMES OF 1984
MUST TAKE PLACE IN GREECE

New York. Athens News Agency

Today's "New York Times" contain a leader in which

the Moscow Olympics is commented upon as the Games with the least participation of nations. In addition the paper blames the situation on the Soviet invasion of Aphganistan. The leading article concludes: "Undoubtedly, this deplorable state of affairs shows that politics must stay out of athletic games. There is one way to come round this problem. Greece, the birthplace of the Olympic Games, must become the permanent site of the Olympiads. The area in Olympia is perfectly available and the government has offered to create an Olympic city under international supervision. The United States can play an important role in this direction, by agreeing to move the 1984 Games to Greece. The Games belong to Greece. It is high time we carried them there".

10. KEY TERMS OF THE ANCIENT GREEK OLYMPIC GAMES

A

Aethlios: Mythical figure, a son of Zeus and Protogeneia; first king of Elis. It is interesting to note that "athletes" were named for Aethlios.

Agon: God in ancient Greece, protector of athletic events, whose artistic illustrations vary greatly, depending on the specific sport that he was assumed to protect.

Alexander: First king of Macedonia who, after managing to prove that he was of Greek origin and, in particular, of the city of Argos, took part in the Games. It should be remembered that only Greeks were allowed to participate in the Games.

Altis: Sacred grove in Olympia, dedicated to Zeus. Within the Altis were included:
1) The temple of Zeus
2) the Heraion
3) the Pelopeion
4) the Metroon
    Further, within the Altis were:
1) the statues of the Olympic victors
2) the stoa of Echo
3) the treasuries of the cities
4) the Prytaneio

Later, the Philippeion and the exedra of Herodes Atticus were built.

Also, within the Altis were statues of Zeus, Hera, Athena, Demeter, Themis, Apollo, Artemis, Hesperides and Nike. All these statues were made of gold and ivory.

Alpheios: River crossing the valley of Olympia. In mythology, Alpheios was a hero, who later was transformed into a river.

Amaltheia: A mythological goat that raised Zeus after he was left by his mother, Rea, in the fort of Ide.

Anolympiads: Void Olympiads organized by the Pisatans, Arcadians on their allies.

Alytai: Special police officers in charge of ensuring the smooth running of the Games.

C

Charioteer: The person who holds the reins and leads the chariot.

Coubertin: French idealist and humanist who worked hard to revive the modern Olympics, an achievement that he performed in 1896.

D

Derpfeld, William: German architect, one of the first researchers who showed interest in the excavations of Olympia. He was awarded the highest Greek medal by the Greek state as a thanksgiving gesture for his contribution to the archaeological research of ancient Greece. His bust was placed, in the museum of Olympia, across that of Ernest Kurt.

E

Ekecheiria: Literally, this terms means in Greek "holding of hands"; it signifies the sacred truce that was observed during the Games by the Greek cities that took part in the Olympiad.

G

Gaia: Godess of ancient Greece; personification of the Earth; mother of the Giants, Titans, Cyclops and others.

Gaion: Sanctuary in which Uranus and Gaia were worshipped.

H

Halteres: Jumping weights, that is stone, iron or lead weights that the athletes held in each hand while the jumped, in order to balance better their body and improve their performance.

Hellanodikai: The official judges of the Games. They had the power impose financial and corporal punishment, to exlude athletes, and in general to apply the rules and regulations of the Olympic Games. They held office for one Olympiad and got formal instruction on their duties for a period of ten months. During their training period they lived in a specially constructed building, the **Hellanodikaion.**

Hercules: The well known hero of the Greek mythology who went to Elis to perform the feat known as "the cleansing of the stables of Augeus".

Heraia: A series of races specifically for girls; they took place every four years at Olympia but were absolutely independent of the Games.

Heraion: An ancient wooden temple dedicated to Hera.

Hermes: Famous statue, a creation of the eminent ancient Greek sculptor Praxiteles. It was found in the Heraion in 1877. It shows Hermes holding the infant god Dionysos in his left arm. Hermes held, probably, in his right hand (which was not found) a bunch of grapes, while the child-god Dionysos reaches out to get the fruit.

Hippodameia: A daughter of Oinomaos, the king of Pisa, and wife of Pelops, the king of Peloponese. She instituted the Heraia, a race for girls.

Hieromenia: The time interval between shortly before the beginning of the Games and shortly after the end of the Games.

I

Idaian Herakles: According to a legend he is referred to as the first to determine the length of the stadium of Olympia.

Iphitos: King of the Eleans, a descendant of Oxylos and leader of the Aitoloi. In common with Lykourgos, king of Sparta, Iphitos agreed the sacred truce in 884 B.C.

K

Kolotos: A pupil of Pheidias, the great Athenian sculptor.

Kouretes: The Kouretes of Idaian Daktyloi were Kretan warriors and priests who moved from Krete to the valley of Olympia.

Kronion: A hill in Olympia, north of the sanctuary of Zeus. According to Pindar, the hill was named Kronion by Herakles after the establishment of the Games.

Kronos: Ancient Greek god, a son of Uranus and Gaia, husband of Rea and father of Zeus, Poseidon, Hera, Demeter, etc.
The cult of Kronos was introduced very early in ancient Creece.

Kurt, Ernest: German archaeologist, Professor of Archaeology at the German School of Archaeology, a prolific author of ancient Greek history and the person in charge of the excavations that began in 1875 and brought to surface ancient Olympia.

Kyniska: The first woman Olympic victor that was crowned after her horses won an equestrian event in the Olympic Games. Her victories were represented into two sculptures that are preserved at Olympia and Sparta, respectively.

M

Myrtilos: Charioteer that was killed by Pelops in the famous chariot race between Oinomaos and Pelops.

N

Nero: Emperor of Rome who was repeatedly declared Olympic victor after buying off or intimidating his opponents or the judges.

O

Olympia: This is the name of the whole area of ancient Pisa. It covered the region that is encircled by the Kronion hill and the rivers Alpheios and Kladeos. It used to be one of the most famous religious centers in the whole of the antiquity. It is the place in which the Olympics, the most important panhellenic athletic events used to take place. It was dedicated to the worship of Olympian Zeus.

Olympiad: The time interval from the end of the Games to the beginning of the fifth year after, that is to the beginning of the next Games. However, another use of the term Olympiad equates the Olympiad with the Olympic Games.

Olympos: A hill located behind the Kronion mountain. It should not be confused with the Olympus of Thessaly.

Oinomaos: King of Pisa who determined that only the man who beat him in a chariot race would qualify as husband for his daughter, Hippodameia.

Orsippos: A runner from Megara, who is said to have been the first athlete to run absolutely naked.

P

Pankration: A very difficult sport, a combination of boxing and wrestling.

Pankratiast: Any athlete of the pankration.

Pausanias: A most famous peregrinator and historian. He was absolutely charmed by the pieces of art that he saw at Olympia and described many of them in much detail.

Pelasgoi: The earliest inhabitants of Elis. The worshipped the elements of nature and established the sanctuary "Gaion".

Pelops: King of Peloponese who beat the king of Pisa Oinomaos and as a result married Pelops' daughter, Hippodameia.

Pisa: Ancient city of Elis, east of Olympia. Originally, they under took the administration and organization of the Games of which the became official chairmen in 748 B.C. They lost this privilege in 364 B.C., after being attacked by the Aitoloi.

Pisatans: The inhabitants of Pisa.

Praxiteles: Great Athenian sculptor of the 4th century B.C. His most famous work was the famous Hermes.

R

Running: One of the most respected sports in the whole of antiquity. The quality of swiftness of foot was so highly valued because of its importance during wars.

S

Spondophoroi: Heralds who prior to the Games used to be sent throughout Greece to declare the sacred armistice and to invite the athletes to take part in the Olympiad.

T

Theokoloi: Priests who lived permanently in Olympia and were responsible for the good maintenance of the sanctuary, the statues etc.

Theodosius: Byzantine emperor who abolished officially the Olympic Games in A.D. 393.

Theoroi: Eminent citizens that were sent by the various cities as official representatives at Olympia.

Tiberius: Eminent Roman who won the equestrian event of "tethrippon" in an Olympiad, under the name Tiberious Claudius Nero.

Triakter: In order to be declared victor in upright wrestling, a wrestler was required to throw his opponent to the ground three times and was therefore called triakter.

Typaion: Precipitous mountain located beyond the Alpheios river. From this mountain used to be thrown the women who violated the prevailing rules and entered the stadium to watch the Games. However, this rule was violated only once, by Pherenike, a daughter of Diagoras.

V

Varasdates: A descendant of the Arsakides; the last Olympic victor of the 291st Olympiad (A.D. 385).

Velestiche: Eminent woman of Macedonian origin who won in the equestrian events at the Games.

Vinkelman: German archaeologist who showed great interest in excavating Olympia but failed to materialize his plans.

Z

Zanes: Copper statues of Zeus the construction of which was financed with the revence from the fines imposed on those who violated the rules of the Games.

Zeus: The father of gods and humans. An altar dedicated to the worship of Zeus was located in the sanctuary of Olympia.

11. COMMEMORATIVE STAMPS AND POSTERS OF THE MODERN OLYMPIADS

1. 1896 OLYMPIC GAMES (ATHENS)

2. 1906 OLYMPIC GAMES (ATHENS)

3. 1912 OLYMPIC GAMES (STOCKHOLM)

4. 1920 OLYMPIC GAMES (ANTWERP)

5. 1924 OLYMPIC GAMES (PARIS)

6. 1928 OLYMPIC GAMES (AMSTERDAM)

7. 1932 OLYMPIC GAMES (LOS ANGELES

8. 1936 OLYMPIC GAMES (BERLIN)

Propagandablatt in japanischer Sprache.

Deutsches Olympia-Ehrenzeichen
erster Klasse

Olympia-Erinnerungsplakette
Vorderseite

Olympia-Erinnerungsplakette
Rückseite

9. 1948 OLYMPIC GAMES (LONDON)

10. 1952 OLYMPIC GAMES (HELSINKI)

11. 1956 OLYMPIC GAMES (MELBOURNE)

12. 1960 OLYMPIC GAMES (ROME)

JEUX DE LA XVII OLYMPIADE
ROMA · 25.VIII–11.IX
ROMA MCMLX

13. 1964 OLYMPIC GAMES (TOKYO)

ΕΛΛΑΣ ΔΡ.1

ΕΛΛΑΣ ΔΡ.2

ΕΛΛΑΣ ΔΡ.2.50

ΕΛΛΑΣ ΔΡ.6

14. 1968 OLYMPIC GAMES (MEXICO)

15. 1972 OLYMPIC GAMES (MUNICH)

16. 1976 OLYMPIC GAMES (MONTREAL)

17. 1980 OLYMPIC GAMES (MOSCOW)

Former Olympic victor Diagoras carried on the shoulders of his two sons.

The Olympia Zeus

Pierre de Coubertin. The man who helped revive the Olympic Games.

BIBLIOGRAPHY

1. *"The Olympic Games 776 B.C. — 1896 A.D.",* by S. Lambros and N. Politis, Athens, 1896.
2. *"Olympia",* by S. Kallisperi, Athens, 1896.
3. *"Olympia",* by V. Leonardos, Athens, 1901.
4. *"A guide to Ancient Olympia",* by Kourniotis, Athens, 1904.
5. *"Esperini",* newspaper, Athens, 1906.
6. *"Astrapi",* newspaper, Athens, 1906.
7. *"The country of the Olympian gods"* by A. Z. Makatounis.
8. *"The Games through the ages"* by N. Alexopoulos, Kalamai, 1930.
9. *"Olympiaka"* by N. Kyparisses, Athens 1934.
10. *"Athletic games and their contribution to the development of international relations",* by G. P. Bacouros, Athens, 1948.
11. *"The Ancient Olympia",* by P. Nikolopoylos, Patras, 1954.
12. *"Olympia",* by Z. Papamihalopoulos, Athens, 1960.
13. *"The Eleaka by Pausanias",* Volume I.
14. *"The Eleaka by Pausanias",* Volume II.

15. *"Homer's Iliad"*.
16. *"Homer's Odyssey"*.
17. *"The Great Greek Encyclopedia"*.
18. *"Helios"*, Encyclopedic Dictionary.
19. *"The modern internatioanal Olympic Games"* by I. Chrisaphis.
20. *"Greece and Games"*, by G. Sakellariou, Athens, 1947.
21. *"Greek Encyclopedia"* by X. Giovanis.
22. *"Domi"*, Greek Encyclopedia.
23. *"Olympia"* by Stratis Myrivelis.
24. *"Great American Encyclopedia"*.
25. *"BAND 1 DIE OLYMPISCHEN WINTERSPIELE VOR-SCHAU AUF BERLIN"* Olympia, 1936.

CONTENTS